UITGAVEN VAN HET
NEDERLANDS HISTORISCH-ARCHAEOLOGISCH INSTITUUT TE ISTANBUL

Publications de l'Institut historique et archéologique néerlandais de Stamboul
sous la direction de
E. VAN DONZEL, Pauline H.E. DONCEEL-VOÛTE,
A.A. KAMPMAN, Machteld J. MELLINK et C. NIJLAND

XLI

CHRISTIAN SEALS OF THE SASANIAN PERIOD

CHRISTIAN SEALS
OF THE SASANIAN PERIOD

by

JUDITH A. LERNER

NEDERLANDS HISTORISCH-ARCHAEOLOGISCH INSTITUUT
TE ISTANBUL
1977

I.S.B.N. 90 6258 041 6
Printed in Belgium

To
D.A. and A.F.R.

PREFACE

I wish to express my sincere thanks to Ernst Kitzinger and Oleg Grabar for reading this work in manuscript and offering many helpful suggestions and additions. I am also grateful to those private collectors and curators who so generously allowed me to study and publish the seals in their keeping: in particular, P. Amiet, Musée du Louvre, Paris; K. Brisch and J. Kröger, Museum für Islamische Kunst, West-Berlin; R. Camber, The British Museum, London; R. Curiel, Bibliothèque Nationale, Paris; M. Foroughi, Teheran; P.O. Harper, The Metropolitan Museum of Art, New York; V.C. Lukonin, State Hermitage Museum, Leningrad; P.R.S. Moorey, Ashmolean Museum, Oxford; R. Noll and W. Oberleitner, Kunsthistorisches Museum, Vienna.

TABLE OF CONTENTS

INTRODUCTION*

Christians living under Persian rule have long been of interest
to students of Sasanian culture. Their communities had been
formed primarily by those Christians who were among the Syrian
captives that the Sasanian kings had resettled in Iran, those
who had sought the protection of the Sasanian crown during the
Monophysite and Nestorian persecutions, or those who had found
themselves under Sasanian rule with the rise and subsequent expansion of the empire throughout Iran and into Mesopotamia between the third and seventh centuries A.D.[1] Written sources
provide information on their economic and social impact, yet
little material evidence of this minority group has been available to reveal their effect upon and interaction with Sasanian
culture, or their similarities and differences with their
brethren to the west. Excavations in Mesopotamia, at Ctesiphon
and Hīra, have revealed Christina churches,[2] while in Iran,
traces of Christian communities have been found on the Island
of Khārg in the Persian Gulf, northwest of Bushīre, dating to
the third century,[3] and at ninth- to eleventh-century Nīshāpūr
in Khorāsān.[4] Further evidence consists of engraved stone seals
which are Sasanian in their form and style and which may be
identified by their motifs as having belonged to Christians.

These seals occur in various collections, mainly without origi-
nal provenance. Their inscriptions sometimes are in Syriac, the
language of the Monophysite and Nestorian Churches, and a few,
actually post-Sasanian though included here, have Kufic writing;
but more commonly they are in Pahlavi or Middle Persian.
Curiously, the people named in these Pahlavi inscriptions bear
good Iranian names, while the rest of the legend or the entire
inscription of a seal is usually a standard Zoroastrian formula. In his catalogue of the cameos and gems in the Bibliothèque Nationale, written in 1858, A. Chabouillet identified five

intaglios as "pierres chrétiennes de l'Asie" (Nos. 1330-1334),
and dated them prior to the Christian persecution of Shāpūr II
in 340.[5] His attribution was followed by C.W. King in his works
on Gnostic remains (1864) and antique gem stones (1872), but
King recognized only Nos. 1330-1333 as "signets of Christianized
Persians", and saw the inscription of No. 1332 (our 25*) as
dating the group after Shāpūr II.[6] Writing in 1899, Ja.I.
Smirnov accepted with some reservations Chabouillet's identifi-
cations, stating that only Nos. 1330-1332 could be of definite
Persian Christian origin.[7] Persian ·seals with Christian motifs
were also recognized by D. Osborne (1912)[8] and a seal in the
British Museum, decorated with a cross (11*), had been discussed by E. Thomas in 1852.[9] Little else about such seals had
been written until A.Ja. Borisov's 1939 publication of a group
of Christian gems in the Oriental Section of the State Hermitage Museum, Leningrad.[10] Borisov's ideas were incorporated by
V.G. Lukonin in the Hermitage catalogue of the Sasanian seal
collection that was published in 1963. In the more recent catalogue of the Sasanian seals in the British Museum, A.D.H. Bivar
discussed the attribution of certain seals to Christian ownership. He thus interpreted 1* and 11* with their prominent
crosses as Christian, but stated that he had not yet seen a
seal for which a Christian interpretation was "unequivocally
confirmed by the inscription". Nonetheless, he thought that
such an interpretation was an entirely natural one.[11]

Certainly those seals (1*-13) on which the cross is the main
motif may be classified as Christian, as may be other seals on
which crosses serve as subsidiary and identifying motifs (14*,
15*, 17*, 20*-24*). Still other seals with images such as those
identified by Chabouillet-the Sacrifice of Isaac, the Visitation, the Virgin and Child - present problems of identification,
for their similarity to traditional Sasanian types tends to
conceal their Christian meaning.

In this monograph I will discuss a group of seals, most of

which I believe to depict Christian motifs and hence would have
belonged to members of Christian communities within the Sasanian domain; other seals in the group appear to lend their decoration to a Christian interpretation. This compilation is not
a corpus; I hope that its publication will stimulate further
investigation into the material remains and iconography of
these Sasanian Christian groups, that other Christian motifs
will be identified, and that the stylistic affinities of these
presumed Christian objects will become better known. My discussion of the seals will begin with the most obvious Christian
image, the cross, and proceed to the identification of typically Christian iconographic motifs: angels, orants, and events
from the New Testament (the Visitation, the Adoration and the
Entry into Jerusalem). It will conclude with two Old Testament
subjects that had great meaning for early Christians, the Sacrifice of Isaac and Daniel in the Lions' Den. As significant
episodes in Jewish art of the same period, the problem of a
Jewish rather than Christian attribution for this last group of
seals will be considered.

Most of the seals are anepigraphic. Those with inscriptions
contribute no positive evidence of their Christian affiliation,
but provide information for the social history of Persian
Christians. Prof. Richard N. Frye has examined the Pahlavi
inscriptions; his readings are appended here, after a catalogue
of the seals (1*-65*).

I. Crosses (1*-14*)

Different types of crosses appear on seals of definite Sasanian
manufacture, and on those for which we can only suggest an origin within the Sasanian political or cultural sphere. The types
are variants of either the Latin cross with elongated lower
arm, or the Greek cross, which has arms of equal length.

A Latin cross with triangular arms that join at their apexes is

associated on two seals with Pahlavi inscriptions of the sixth
to seventh centuries (1* and 2*).[12] This is a common form of
cross which occurs on objects of East Christian and Persian
provenance, specifically on square and hexagonal glass flasks
of probable Palestinian manufacture. These vessels most likely
date to the fifth and sixth centuries, and have been found as
far east as Rayy in central Iran.[13] A silver dish owned by R.
Ettinghausen is decorated on its interior with a similar cross
that is set upon a stepped base.[14] The elongated shape of the
vessel is attested as early as the fifth century at Balalyk
Tepe in Central Asia.[15]

The crosses of the seals and the dish are related to the cross
with expanding extremities which was widespread throughout Byzantine times. As early as the fifth century, it appears in the
apse mosaic of Sta. Pudenziana in Rome where it is thought to
represent the jewelled cross erected on Golgotha by Theodosius
II (408-450).[16] With the coinage of Tiberius II (578-582),
this cross appears on a stepped platform[17] and becomes a standard iconographic form with its adoption by Heraclius (610-
641).[18] The use in the West of the cross potent on steps helps
to date the silver dish; sometime after the fifth century would
be appropriate and it would be also for the seals. Prior to
Heraclius' adoption of the Golgotha cross, it had appeared,
with expanding or flaring arms, and punctuated by teardrops or
jewels, on the sixth-century Palestinian lead ampullae now at
Monza and Bobbio,[19] in a fresco in a mausoleum in Sofia,[20] and
on the silver plate, of Syrian origin, found in the Perm region
and now in Leningrad.[21]

On the Perm plate the cross rests on a starry globe which also
symbolizes the cross on Golgotha;[22] in the crucifixion scene on
Monza ampulla 5, the cross also rests upon a globe which, in
turn, stands on the rocky hill of Golgotha.[23] In a similar
fashion, the cross appears above a globe on a bezel in the
Bibliothèque Nationale(3*). A single line sharply delineates

the slightly flaring arms of the cross, while two fainter ones join the globe to the lowest arm. A crescent and six-pointed star flank this lower extremity, while late Pahlavi inscriptions run down either side of the entire cross. Sasanian coins of a modified Byzantine type, struck in Alexandria during its occupation between 619 and 629, depict on their reverses the cross with expanding arms upon a globe.[24] On the obverses, the frontal bust of the emperor, wearing a cross and crescent-topped crown, is flanked by a six-pointed star and crescent. The crescent is on end, with its horn facing outwards to the rim of the coin, but on the seal the horns are upright. On some of the Palestinian ampullae, the cross of the Crucifixion is flanked by the sun and moon above its horizontal arm. By their placement, the star and crescent on the seal appear to serve as a decorative device, well within the tradition of Sasanian coinage and glyptic art.[25]

A variation of the cross with expanding arms occurs on Monza ampulla 4: the cross, set on its stepped base, has its dotted extremities actually splayed or bifurcated.[26] This exaggeration of the extremities also occurs on some of the Syrian cruets; the arms are not dotted and the long arm ends in the stepped base or a globe.[27] This bifurcated type without dotted ends appears on two Pahlavi-inscribed seals in Berlin(4) and in the S.Y. Nayeri Collection, Tadjrish, Iran(5). The type continues in Iran into post-Sasanian times when it decorates the interior of a bowl, perhaps from Nīshāpūr,[28] as does the bifurcated type with dotted ends.[29]

A more widespread version of the Latin cross with bifurcated ends is found on some seals, all but one known to me, forming a distinct group by their material, shape, and inscriptions (6*-11*). The dotted splayed ends of the crosses on these seals are embellished with a larger circle or globe that is set between each pair of dots. The resulting trilobed shape of the extremities is absent from 9* which is due to its cursory rendering

which lengthens or eliminates the two dots at the ends to
create a sharp bifurcation. The large circle or globe at the
lower end of the vertical arm corresponds to the globe of 3*,
and in 6* and 11* rests upon a base. On all but one of these
seals, a legend runs vertically to either side of the lower arm
of the cross; that of 6* and 7* is written in Syriac, while
that of 8-10 is in Kufic. On 11* the inscription continues
around the base of the cross and is in Pahlavi. The Syriac-
and Kufic-inscribed seals are of rock crystal, roughly conical
in shape with four flattened sides and a slightly convex base
which bears the intaglio. The Pahlavi seal is of chalcedony,
and, as described by Bivar, is a "necked" or hollow cabochon
stamp.

Crosses with trefoliated ends decorate an inkwell from post-
Sasanian Nīshāpūr,[30] as well as a group of stone slabs that
were dedicated at various sites in southern India by a member
of a local Persian Nestorian community.[31] These have been dated
by their Pahlavi inscription between the sixth and ninth centuries. But the cross on the seals, with its splayed tips and
distinct globe between them, is not trefoliated; rather, it is
closer to a cross form that appears on one of the sixth-century
Bobbio ampullae fragments, and on later objects and architectural decoration.[32] On the ampulla fragment, the arms of the
cross consist of palm trunks of leaves which naturally branch
outward to form its four bifurcated ends; nesting within each
fork is a large globe.[33] A similar configuration that no longer
treats the arms as vegetal elements is seen on a fragmentary
stucco plaque from one of the churches at Hīra;[34] and also
appears in mosaic in the Church of the Nativity in Bethlehem.[35]

A true parallel to the cross on the seals occurs at Hīra,
painted on the chapel wall of the church in mound XI.[36] This
phase of the church was dated by D. Talbot Rice to the seventh
century and thus provides a likely date for the seals. The
Syro-Mesopotamian origin of the rock crystal seals that is sug-

gested by the painted cross at Hīra finds additional confirma-
tion in their Syriac and Kufic inscriptions, as well as in
their traditional Mesopotamian shape.[37] Although the Syriac-
inscribed seals may be post-Sasanian, as indeed are their Kufic
relatives, the series certainly begins in at least late Sasanian times with seal 11*.

Another Latin cross (12*) displays an extremely long lower arm
with a short horizontal stroke at each end. A circular blob
fills in the right angle of the join above the cross bar, while
the lower quadrants of the cross are filled by the upturned
ends of a ribbon. This ribbon is tied about the middle of the
lower arm in the manner of certain Sasanian representations of
fire-altars,[38] and so marks the cross - and hence the seal itself - as a distinctly Sasanian product. The ribbon recalls the
curving palmettes or volutes that grow from the bases of the
Nestorian Indian crosses and which may be associated with the
leafy growths that begin to decorate crosses in the seventh
century or earlier.[39] Such "leaved crosses" are found among the
eighth-century stucco plaques from Hīra,[40] on an earthenware
plaque from ninth- or tenth-century Nīshāpūr,[41] and are common
by the ninth century and later on Italian, Armenian and Byzantine monuments.[42] They are thought by Rice to be of Nestorian
origin and to have spread from Mesopotamia to reach their subsequent elaborate development. The ribbon attachment on the Sasanian seal may be a Persian translation of the leafy decoration. Certainly, it is a typically Persian interpretation of
this Christian symbol.

The cross of 12* stands within an undecorated arch that is sup-
ported by two short columns. This is in many respects identical
to the arch that shelters the cross on some of the Palestinian
ampullae. The arch has been interpreted by André Grabar as an
honorific device, used to indicate the triumphal nature of the
cross and not as a specific reference to that erected on Golgotha.[43] The combination of the arch and the tied ribbon emphasi-

zes the venerative aspect of the cross on this seal.

The Greek cross with arms of equal length decorates a seal in East Berlin (13). A short perpendicular stroke terminates each arm. Above the cross is a short horizontal bar, and below it the Sasanian ribbon emerges from either side of an ovoid shape. This is the only Sasanian seal that I know on which the cross with arms of equal length is the main subject. Usually it appears in the field, not merely as a filling motif, but as an indication of the Christian ownership of the seal. Thus, it occurs on a hemispherical seal in the Bibliothèque Nationale as an adjunct to a double-line inscription in Syriac letters (14*: the cross on the bottom in the seal inpression has arms of equal length; that on the top may be intentionally a Latin cross but most likely represents a slip by the seal-engraver). Small crosses decorate coin reverses of Justinian (527-565), [44] but the idea of filling devices is common enough to Sasanian glyptic design not to be considered here as a chronological indicator. Additional instances of the Greek cross as a secondary device, used to indicate the Christian nature of certain seals, will be encountered later.

II. Figures Associated with the Cross (15*-24*)
A. Angels (15*)

On a hemispherical stamp in the British Museum, two confronted angels raise between them a wreath in order to crown a Latin cross. Their legs are bent sharply at the knee as if they were kneeling to either side of the cross, but they could also be hovering in the air. Along the lower edge of the seal, below the angels' legs and the cross, is a late, perhaps sixth-century, Pahlavi inscription. Each arm of the cross ends in a short perpendicular stroke. A short horizontal line bisects the lower arm and may mark the actual termination of that member. If so, the extension beneath it could represent the platform upon which the cross rests. Steps are not indicated but this is in keeping with the summary treatment of the entire design. The cross thus depicted could be the commemorative cross erected on Golgotha, glorified by the angels and their wreath.

Angels that flank the cross or bear it within a wreath between them is a familiar image in Coptic and Byzantine art from the fourth century on, but I know of no example where angels actually crown it.[45] The style of the carving - similar to the late Sasanian "stressed manner" - eliminates from the figures details of headdress and costume, and so precludes one possible aspect of their association with western angels. The position of their legs, with the far one above and parallel with the near one, is characteristic of western representations, although in western examples, the hem of the long robe appears at the ankles. The absence of a hemline, along with the clear delineation of a pair of legs for each figure creates the impression that the angels are naked; however, a transparent robe may have been intended.

B. Humans (16 *-24 *)
1. Man holding a cross (16 *-19 *)

The four seals to be discussed each depict a male personage, facing to the right and holding before him a long, cross-shaped staff. All but the man on 19 * wear a long robe that flares at the hem, and, as shown on 16 *-18 *, is bound at the waist by a belt; 19 * is too cursory to make out the style of garment. This long robe is atypical for a Sasanian man, the standard Persian male dress being a tunic or jacket with trousers. The robe is not so unusual in a Christian context, however, for it closely resembles the long tunic that is worn by orants and other figures in Christian representations. In fact, the diagonal folds on the lower portion of the robe (16 *-18 *) are found on the garment of the personage who holds a cross on the Byzantine intaglio in Figure A;[46] the diagonal gathers on his robe are not made by a belt but by a mantle or broad scarf that has been wrapped around his body and draped over one shoulder. Similarly, the curved shapes that hang down the back of the man on 17* do not represent wings as Borisov and Lukonin had thought, but cloth, and thus must be a scarf with twisted ends. The double ends probably indicate that the scarf is draped over both shoulders in the manner of the stola worn by the orant saint in a sixth-century Coptic painting from Saqqara (Fig. B).[47]

Behind the cross-bearer on 17* is a small cross with arms of equal length which may serve to reiterate his Christian affiliation. Both 16* and 18* bear Pahlavi legends, that of 16* is extremely interesting since, according to Bivar, it may refer to the city of Bīshāpūr in Fārs. This priestly figure could have been associated with a Christian community there,[48] and, indeed, Christians were among the Syrian prisoners of war that were resettled in Fārs and other provinces.[49]

A parallel in Byzantine art to the long-robed figure with the long cross is the coin reverse of Victory, in tunic and toga-like mantle, facing left and supporting in her right hand a large jewelled cross. The type first appears in the early fifth century on the solidi of Theodosius II and his wife Eudocia,[50] and continues until Justin I (518-527) when Victory is transformed into an archangel who appears in full-face with both the long cross and a globe surmounted by a small cross.[51] As a popular motif for Christian intaglio designs, the Victory-Archangel usually is shown holding the long cross.[52]

2. Man in prayer; orant (20*-23*)

Two seals in the collections of M. Foroughi, Teheran and the University Museum, Philadelphia (20* and 21) depict a male personage, facing to the right, with both arms raised before him in a reverential gesture. This gesture with palms open towards the worshipper is seen frequently on Sasanian seal representations of worshippers before an altar or holding a barsom

bundle;[53] on 20* an altar appears behind the worshipper. There
is nothing to indicate that these seals are exclusively Christian, except for the men's dress and the crosses in the field.
The garment worn by the man on 20* is similar to that on 16*,
and identical to that of an orant saint on an early Byzantine
seal.[54] This latter figure wears a long tunic and long scarf
which is wound about him to create diagonal folds from his left
hip to his right knee, while leaving both ends free to hang
down his back, where they appear to either side of his torso.
This arrangement, according to Campbell Bonner, resembles that
shown on certain ivory carvings of the early sixth century.[55]
The dress of the worshipper on 21 appears to be the long belted
robe that is worn by the men with cross-shaped staffs.

The crosses that appear in the field - on 20*, one before the
worshipper, another behind him, above the altar; on 21, two to
either side of the figure - are the type with arms of equal
length, but they lack the short perpendicular stroke at each
end that characterizes the Greek crosses on 13 and 14*. Such
simple crosses without perpendicular terminations decorate many
Sasanian seals; they appear above a fire altar, as on 20*,
which is often approached by a worshipper of probable Zoroastrian persuasion,[56] or they flank as well as surmount a fire
altar.[57]

Smirnov believes that the appearance on a seal of the Greek
cross with perpendicular terminations indicated its Christian
ownership, even if its subject is a lion or another typical Sasanian motif.[58] Whether the plain cross on 20* with arms of
equal length and without these terminations should also be considered an exclusively Christian device is uncertain for it too
flanks a walking lion,[59] a frontal male portrait bust,[60] appears
in association with a "monogram" design[61] and before a Sasanian
lady who characteristically holds a flower to her nose.[62] Yet
it also is associated on seals with orants and with other subjects that are possibly Christian (25* and 57*).

On 22* and 23* a man in a belted tunic appears with arms raised,
palms out, to either side of his body. This is the orans attitude of Christian worshippers (Fig. B), and is never employed
by Zoroastrian devotees. But, unlike most western orants and in
keeping with Sasanian convention, the figures are not completely frontal: that on 22* would be except for the profile head,
while that on 23* has both head and feet in profile. The dress
of these worshippers may be related to the long robe of the
staff-bearers, although the garment of 22* seems to end below
the knee and thus is similar to the garment of the Sasanian
worshipper cited in note 56. Small crosses with equal arms
flank both figures, the position of the four on 23* being identical with those on 21. Identically-placed crosses are commonly
associated with western orants (Fig. B).[63] Both 22* and 23* are
inscribed in Pahlavi with the standard Zoroastrian apastan formula.

C. Couple with Crosses Between Them (24*)

On a nicolo bezel in the Bibliothèque Nationale, the busts of a
man and a woman face each other. Her left arm and his right are
included, hers raised in reverence towards the ribboned cross
that seems to float above and between them, his, also raised in
that direction, but also holding an object which may be a cross
with strongly flaring arms. Below and also between them, is yet
another cross, identical to the first but without the ribbon
embellishment. The couple displays the usual Sasanian physiog-
nomy and dress; the way in which the man grasps the cross between his thumb and index finger is a typically Sasanian gesture found on many portraits and other gems where the subject
holds a flower.[64] A Pahlavi inscription - which includes the
apastan formula - runs completely around the edge. The ribboned
cross is the same type as on 12* which we saw as honorific in
nature, and this is confirmed on 24* by the gestures of the
couple.[65]

Other Sasanian seals depict the confronted busts of a man and a woman,[66] and Bivar has suggested, following F.H. Marshall on Roman intaglios, that the juxtaposed portraits of a man and woman are to be connected with marriage rites.[67] Since the double or triple portraits on Roman imperial coinage which expressed the marital and parental ties of the emperor were also imitated by the Sasanian kings on their coins,[68] it is not unreasonable to assume that the double portrait seals also expressed a family or matrimonial relationship. Gold marrige rings with the busts of the couple and a cross between them, often inscribed in Greek with the couple's names or the words "Grace of God" or "Concord", are known from Constantinple, as well as from the western part of the Byzantine Empire.[69] On those of the late fourth or early fifth century the busts are confronted, in profile, as on our seal, while on those of the sixth and certainly of the seventh centuries, the busts are in full-face.[70] Our seal thus appears to have been part of a matrimonial ring that belonged to Christians living under Sasanian rule, and to have been "Iranized" by its style, the ribboned cross, and the substitution of a Zoroastrian invocation for the usual Greek one.

III. New Testament Subjects (25*-30*)
A. The Visitation (25*- 27*)

25*, in the Bibliothèque Nationale, was described by Chabouillet as "St. Elizabeth and the Virgin facing each other, holding hands; between them a star and crescent. Pahlavi inscription;[71] this last element is the apastan formula. 26* and 27*, also depicting two confronted women with a cross between them, perhaps should be similarly interpreted, as did C.W. King in regard to 26*.[72] The motif is rare in Sasanian art. It is far more usual for two men, a man and a woman, or a man and a statue of a goddess to stand opposite each other.[73]

The Visitation is an important episode in Early Christian doctrine. In evangelical cycles it is shown immediately before the Nativity as the first recognition of Christ: Elizabeth, pregnant

with John the Baptist, greets Mary with an embrace and is the
first to proclaim the divinity of the child in Mary's womb.[74]
The scene cannot be traced earlier than to the fifth century,
and its depiction as an embrace, not until the sixth.[75] The two
women need not envelop each other, but, as on some of the Palestinian ampullae, rush towards each other and clasp hands.[76]
This, in fact, is the gesture of the women on 25*, even though
their bodies are completely stationary and no movement is im-
plied. Somewhat in contrast, are the women on 26* and 27*.
Their bodies sway towards each other, and on 27*, if not also
on 26*, their outer hands appear to join. The curved protrusion
at their backs may represent a veil which billows out behind
them as on one of the Monza ampullae. The rather stiff rendering
of suspended movement is in accord with the Sasanian style.

The long cross between the women on 27* is supplemented by a
crescent; the small cross with arms of equal length on 25*
shares the space between the pair with the Sasanian star and
crescent. In these contexts the appearance of the crosses is
not definite proof of Christian ownership, while on the basis
of previous examples, the apastan formula of 25* is inconclu-
sive for any attribution. At best, we can only suggest a Christian association for the three seals.

B. Virgin and Child: the Adoration (28*)

A very tentative Christian attribution must be given to a seal
in the Bibliothèque Nationale which depicts a woman in right
profile, seated with a male child on her lap. Identified as the
Virgin and Christ child by Chabouillet, and conditionally accepted as such by Smirnov, no filling motifs provide confirma-
tion, nor does the late Pahlavi inscription. A woman and child
is not an unusual theme in Sasanian glyptic art. On a seal in
the Hermitage, a seated woman holds a child with his body turned
towards her;[77] on one in the British Museum, a child faces in
the same direction as his mother, but in the manner of Sasanian

banqueters, he holds a floral wreath while she reclines on a couch.[78] The child on 28* echoes the strict profile position of his mother, and dangles his feet away from her knees. Their position bears a striking resemblance to early Christian and Byzantine representations of the Virgin and Child in the Adoration of the Magi,[79] and the image on our seal may be an abbreviation of this episode.[80]

Two bezels in the Hermitage also depict a small male figure seated, to the right, on the lap of a woman in the manner of 28*.[81] Although the carving is even cruder than that of 28*, the characterization of the small figure as nude with a band about his head and the woman as wearing a long flounced skirt can be made out in both seals; in place of the double diadem ties that hang down the woman's back on 28*, a single tie or pigtail appears with a bifurcated end. Befitting their poor quality, both seals are anepigraphic; on one, the woman holds a parasol with both hands. The seals are certainly derivative of 28* and must be provincial - perhaps post-Sasanian - products.

A second seal in the Bibliothèque Nationale, 1110[e], attempts to depict a male child seated on a woman's lap, although the extremely crude engraving makes the child float in space. A sixth-century Pahlavi inscription surrounds them, and within its circumference, behind the seated woman, stands a small female figure. The disposition of the figures suggests no Christian connotations.

C. The Entry into Jerusalem (29* and 30*)

The scene on 29* is so identified on the basis of its composition; that on 30* is problematic, but in the light of Sasanian iconography and stylization, I believe the identification is plausible. The Entry began to appear in the fourth century on Christian sarcophagi as the religious or eschatological counterpart of the imperial adventus - a vision of the "First

Coming" of Christ which marks the beginning of the cycle of re-
demption.[82]

On 29* the rider is flanked by a group of three figures, one of
whom in the group on the left raises a hand in salutation. A
cross with arms of equal length appears immediately above each
group, perhaps to indicate the Christian nature of the image,
but its attachment to the figure with the raised arm may also
be a reference to the palm branches that are held by the people
who greet Christ in many representations of this scene.[83] For
example, on a wooden lintel from the Fayyum, two nimbate figures bearing branches flank the mounted Christ;[84] on a seventh-
century gem in The Hague, two pairs of figures stand to either
side of Christ's mount, the innermost one of each pair holding
towards Christ a palm branch,[85] while on a seal in the British
Museum, pairs of figures also greet him, the first in the pair
behind him bearing a palm branch (Fig. C).[86] Like the asses in
these representations, and on the sixth-century ivory diptych
from Etchmiadzin, Armenia,[87] the one on 29* walks without bend-
ing its knees. In Roman depictions such as the sarcophagus of
Junius Bassus, as well as some east Christian ones such as that
in the Rossano Codex, the ass raises its far foreleg. This is
also the usual posture for mounted horses in Sasanian art.[88] It
has been purposely abandoned in 29* to emphasize that the animal is an ass, and thereby further help to identify the seal's
motif. Unlike most oriental or east Christian representations
of the mounted Christ,[89] the rider on 29* is not seated side-
saddle and in full-face; the arc surrounding his head may be
the nimbus that is found in some east Christian representations,
but here it seems to be attached to the rider's arms.

30* is of more typical Sasanian workmanship, and appears to be
an abbreviation of the scene. A rider mounted on a horse with
all four legs on the ground occurs on a seal in the British
Museum,[90] but on our seal, the animal decidedly is an ass or
donkey. As on 29*, the rider is not in full-face, yet he holds

aloft a cross, and thus recalls the Christs of the Etchmiazdin
panel and of an ivory plaque that belongs to the Chair of Maxi-
mian at Ravenna.[91]

The ass and rider fill the entire area of the seal's surface; a
six-pointed star and the Zoroastrian apastan formula complete
its decoration, but, as we have seen, do not necessarily indicate a non-Christian origin. The seal is not the usual Sasanian
ellipsoid or dome with flattened sides as is 29*, but is a
rather thick disk with a transverse perforation. On one side of
the upright edge, between the two drill holes, - and, in relation to the carving on the surface, behind the rider - a palm
branch is incised. This may support our identification for the
palm could symbolize the branches that were spread before Christ
for his ass to walk upon.[92] However, the opposite side of the
edge bears the figure of a reclining zebu bull, a motif which
is more at home in Zoroastrian iconography.

The reverse of the disk also serves as an intaglio, and is decorated with a human eye attacked by various animals and rep-
tiles. The apotropaic image of the Evil Eye is a common amuletic device and frequently serves as a reverse type for the
Syro-Palestinian amulets with a nimbate rider on horseback.[93]
This divine or saintly rider slays various noxious creatures,
and when converted into a Christian hero, is identified as St.
George or St. Sissinius.[94] The association, then, of the "all-
suffering eye" with a Christian scene, specifically the Entry
into Jerusalem which also calls for a mounted figure, is not
strange. The amuletic character of the seal with its four
separately engraved surfaces is charged with additional potency
by the Entry motif. In the Byzantine world, whole cycles of
scenes from the life of Christ were combined on medallions, not
in chronological order, but so as to "recall events that testi-
fy to the saving power of Christ in order to appear for the
same preservation for the wearer of the medallion"; these
medallions attest to the "prophylactic use of evangelical ima-

gery."[95]

IV. Old Testament Subjects (31*-65*)

Two Old Testament episodes can be recognized among Sasanian
seal designs: The Sacrifice of Isaac (Genesis XXII:1-14) and
Daniel in the Lions' Den (Daniel VI:16-23). Both were signifi-
cent in early Christian as well as Jewish iconography as examples of divine deliverance; in both, the participants had de-
monstrated their total faith and trust in God, and thus were
saved.[96] The reliance on Jewish pictorial and literary imagery
for the representation of Old Testament scenes has been noted
by Grabar, Weitzmann and others;[97] the problem of attributing
some of our seals to Jews living within the Sasanian Empire
rather than to Christians will be taken up later.

A. The Sacrifice of Isaac (31*-55*)

This large group of seals which illustrates the Sacrifice of
Isaac by Abraham typically consists of the following elements
essential to the Old Testament narrative: a bearded figure in a
long skirt or a kilt, an altar, and a ram. The most dramatic
moment of the episode, Genesis XXII:10-14, is represented.
Abraham, his knife poised to slay his son, hears the angel of
God call to him and turns to find the ram caught in the thicket
that will replace Isaac as a burnt offering. Thus, on the seals
the bearded figure stands beside the altar with one arm raised
and most typically turns his head towards the ram behind him
(31*-35*, 37*-42*, 46, 52-54).

The most common representation of the scene, 38*-43, 45*-54, is
actually an abbreviation of the sacrifice; 44* is a further
condensation, for the ram is omitted. The subject of these seals
is usually identified as a magus or priest at an altar who is
about to sacrifice the ram behind him,[98] and, indeed, the dress
of the bearded figure often resembles that worn by the Zoroas-

trian worshippers who carry the barsom bundle in other seal depictions.[99] However, more detailed renderings of the episode
leave no doubt that the Sacrifice of Isaac is intended. Chabouillet had so identified 31*, not only by the presence of
of the elements mentioned, but by the body of a child lying on
the altar.[100] On other seals, the child is reduced to a stick
figure, yet remains easily recognizable (32*-34, 36 *and 38*),
while on still other, less carefully carved seals, only some
horizontal markings serve to indicate the body (37*, 39, 44*
and 48). The bush or thicket that entraps the ram is also included on 31* and, by less stylized means, on 32*-35. Chabouillet mistook the bush on 31* for "the angel who shows Abraham
the ram which he restrains by one of its horns".[101] Instead of
the angel, the Hand of God appears above the ram, and it is
actually towards this that Abraham turns his head.

On 55* the Sacrifice of Isaac is unmistakable. Abraham, carefully portrayed as an aged patriarch, lunges with his knife towards his son who is seated upon a rocky knoll; the ram stands
to the left behind Abraham. Both in style and composition this
seal differs from the other Sasanian representations. The execution of the figures, their movement, and the sense of space
created between the main group of Abraham and Isaac, anchored
to the foreground by a groundline, and the isolated figure of
the ram reveal Greco-Roman inspiration. The Pahlavi inscription
above the scene, dated by Frye to the third of fourth century,
places the seal at the beginning of the Sasanian period, at a
time of active artistic influence from the West.[102] Moreover,
its shape is an oval bezel with convex face that was popular in
both Roman and Sasanian regions, but was more widespread in the
former. It seems likely, therefore, that the seal was made by a
western seal-cutter - perhaps a deportee from Syria - and probably then inscribed for its purchaser, a Pahlavi-speaking
Christian. However, the composition of the scene does not
reflect contemporary western depictions.

The rocky promontory upon which Isaac is bound refers to Mount
Moriah, the Biblical setting of the Sacrifice, and, as interpreted by early Christian theologians, the counterpart of Golgotha, the scene of Christ's sacrifice.[103] In early Christian
art, Mount Moriah is depicted only in the catacomb paintings;
but even in these, such as the third-century Capella Greca,
Isaac appears to be kneeling behind the mountain while the
altar is placed to the right of the scene.[104] In all other
Christian representations, including Coptic, Syro-Palestinian
and early Byzantine, the Sacrifice is attempted on or alongside
the altar.[105] The type of altar varies according to the origin
of each representation. A horned or denticulated altar, often
upon a stepped base, appears on the painted dome of a tomb-
chapel at el-Bagawāt,Egypt[106] as well as on a group of ivory
pyxides.[107] The columnar altar with low stepped base and stepped capital that occurs on the Sasanian seals is a type of fire
altar that appears on Sasanian coin reverses of the third
through sixth centuries,[108] and on seals as a separate motif or
as the object of veneration by an acolyte.[109]

On the Sasanian seals, Isaac, when included, lies across the
altar. In most early Christian and Byzantine representations,
Isaac kneels on the ground before the altar. This pose, as
Weitzmann has shown, derives from a classical model, the scene
of the attempted slaying of Orestes in the Telephus of Euripi-
pes.[110] On other Christian monuments Isaac is placed upon the
altar, but he is either seated or kneeling upon it - never
flung across it.[111] The placement of Isaac upon the altar is
faithful to the Biblical account. However, in the earliest por-
trayals of the Sacrifice, those of the catacombs, Isaac often
is not even shown near the altar. Instead, he carries the wood
for his own sacrifice (a reference to Christ carrying the
cross), or he appears as an orant giving thanks for his deliverance. The actual Sacrifice, then, is a later, fourth-
century, addition to Christian iconography, and the appearance
of Isaac lying across the altar in Sasanian representations

does not derive from a known early Christian or Byzantine model.
One other scene of the Sacrifice depicts Isaac actually lying
upon the altar, that on the west wall of the Torah Shrine of
the Synagogue at Dura-Europos (Fig. D).[112] Dated to A.D. 244
by C.H. Kraeling, the painting is a close contemporary of 55*.
Yet certain of its elements show a greater affinity with the
other, and all probably later, Sasanian seals: the position of
Isaac, the raised knife in the hand of Abraham, the ram tether-
ed to the bush, and, as on 31*, the Hand of God.

If 55* is the earliest Sasanian depiction of the Sacrifice, it
must reflect some third-century western model as yet unknown.
By the following century western models were no longer used,
for, as 31*-37*, 45* and 48 show, Isaac appears as he does at
Dura-Europos in what seems to have become a uniquely Sasanian
interpretation of the event.

The development and chronology of the Sacrifice of Isaac in
Sasanian art cannot be established with any certainty, but on
the evidence of the seals certain groupings may be made which
suggest geographical or temporal preferences. A carnelian oval
bezel with flat back and face and a bevelled edge is the most
popular stone and shape, serving for almost half the group
(33*-35, 36*-44*), while the oval shape in other materials is
used for 31*(banded agate), 35*(nicolo) and 46 (almandine).
Carnelian bezels with one convex and one flat surface are used
for 32* and 45*. The characteristically Sasanian ellipsoid
form, also of carnelian, serves for 37*, and agate is used for
40 and 48; an agate hemisphere, also a good Sasanian shape, is
used for 47. The style and quality of execution varies and no
doubt spans at least one century. Only 32* bears an inscription
and this has been dated by Frye to the fifth century. Since 32*
depicts one of the more carefully rendered scenes it perhaps
should be placed towards the beginning of the series. 37*, 47
and 48 are rather carelessly executed and may be later, while
also showing the late adoption of the traditional stamp shapes.

43, a carnelian bezel mounted in a bronze ring, comes from a grave at Mtzkhet-Samtavro, Georgia, where it was found on the right index finger of a female skeleton. It most probably belongs to the sixth century, the date of the Byzantine ring that was on the corresponding finger of the left hand.[113] The perfunctory engraving of 43 is a further indication of a late date. On 43 as well as on 36* and 45*, Abraham looks towards the altar. This represents a late departure from the established composition and the drama of the Biblical story; but all the elements are included to identify the scene as the Sacrifice of Isaac and set it apart from those depictions of a Zoroastrian priest before a fire altar.

49*-54 form another group by their style, material and shape. All are of hematite and are either hemispherical or ellipsoid in shape: on all the scene is starkly delineated. Bold strokes create the figures while certain linear conventions indicate portions of their form, for example, the division of the ram's torso by strokes of parallel lines, and the abstract rendering of Abraham's arms and shoulders as a narrow ellipse. The date of these seals is not known, but they must be from the later part of the Sasanian period, certainly not earlier than the fifth century.

B. Daniel in the Lions' Den (56*-65*)

On these seals a bearded male figure, dresses in a long robe or knee-length kilt, stands between two lions, his body in frontal view and his head in right profile. On 57*-64 his hands are raised and open in the attitude of a Christian orant. On 56* he grasps a cross in each hand, while on 65* his hands are not raised but held in front at his waist. On all these seals, the person depicted recalls the ancient oriental lion-tamer or master of wild beasts, but, unlike that hero, he never touches or holds the animals. His attitude and dress identify him as Daniel,[114] as they do on most other Christian monuments in the

West.

In most of those representations, Daniel is more often naked
than clothed. His earliest appearances, in the catacombs of the
third and fourth centuries, show him between the lions as a nude
orant,[115] a possible reminiscence of the lion-taming Herakles.[116]
On the mid-fourth-century sarcophagus of Junius Bassus, Daniel
is dressed as a classical philosopher in chiton and himation,[117]
but more typically, the clothed Daniel wears a short tunic, to
which is often added trousers, a cloak and the Phrygian cap,
the western version of oriental or Persian dress. The naked
Daniel also occurs on the earliest example of the subject in
glyptic art, a gem dated to the fourth century by a Constanti-
nian monogram on its reverse.[118] On another gems of a slightly
later date, the otherwise naked Daniel wears the Phrygian
cap;[119] in addition, a cross with arms of equal length appears
above each lion's head, to either side of Daniel's raised arms,
in a composition similar to that of 57*. By the fifth century
at Antioch, Daniel appears in full oriental garb - belted tunic,
trousers, cloak and Phrygian cap - in the orant attitude, though
with his head in three-quarter view;[120] while on a Byzantine
cameo of a later date, he is identically dressed and is a completely frontal figure with nimbate head.[121] The Persian costume seems to have become characteristic of fifth- to seventh-
century Byzantine representations, being worn by the Daniels at
Ravenna[122] and on ivory pyxides.[123] This costume has little in
common with the true Persian - or Sasanian - depiction of Daniel.

The Sasanian version of Daniel shows him bare-headed, except
for a fillet which binds his hair in contemporary Persian
fashion. The long garment that he wears on 56*-60 bears some
resemblance to the robes worn by the figures on 16*-21, but
consists of horizontal flounces or bands of ribbing. This
ribbed material, in turn, forms the belted robe that is worn by
a male figure on a Syriac-inscribed seal in the British Museum
(Fig. E).[124] Although J.B. Segal has identified this personage

as a pagan deity whose cult was observed in the Arab-Aramaean regions under Sasanian rule, he offers no conclusive proof,[125] and, by providing Christian parallels for the titles in the seal's inscription, no positive evidence that it could not have Christian affiliations. That the garment is of Syrian and not Persian origin is most likely and is in keeping with the dress of the Christian followers on 16*-21. In fact, Daniel appears in a long belted robe on a silver plate with scenes similar to those on the ampullae as well as on a limestone relief, both of Syrian origin.[126] On 57* Daniel wears an upper garment with long ends hanging to either side below his waist. This may represent the stole that is worn by the Christian worshippers on 20* and in Figure B. The careful carving of 57* further allows us to see that the ribbed garment is gathered at the waist by a girdle, as in Figure E, and that the long sleeves are rolled up at the shoulders to free the arms for action. Such is the garment of the nimbate Daniel on sixth- to eighth-century Byzantine bullae, who stands between the lions as a true orant with both frontal head and body.[127]

The Daniel of 61-65* wears a knee-length skirt or kilt, marked with vertical stripes, and tight-fitting long-sleeved upper garment. This costume is closely related to the dress of the Near Eastern lion-tamer. In late Assyrian and Babylonian times, the standard dress of the hero in animal contest scenes was a short kilt worn beneath a long split skirt, but an animal-tamer also was shown in a simple knee-length skirt or tunic, bound at the waist, and a short-sleeved upper garment.[128] By the Achaemenid period, the preferred lion- or monster-fighter was the Persian king, dressed in his long candys, although occasionally the traditional hero appears in the simple knee-length skirt.[129] On Sasanian seals, this type of skirt is worn by the male worshippers cited in notes 56 and 98, the Abraham on 32*, 34, 35, 47 and 48, as well as by lion-killers who stab the rampant beast with a long spear.[130]

Unlike these lion-fighters and the earlier heroes who firmly grasp their single or paired adversaries by their throats, legs or tails, Daniel never touches the lions. He is portrayed in his capacity of lion-tamer, but, true to the Biblical account, he never appears in actual combat.[131] With the exception of 65*, he is an orant, giving thanks for his deliverance; on 65*, his position recalls that of the Daniel on the Syrian plate, found in the Perm region, which shows the prophet in a kind of exergue, dressed in a long robe, his arms close to his body with his hands turned palms out. The kilted costume that Daniel sometimes wears is perhaps a reminiscence of the more active oriental hero;[132] his long ribbed garment must refer to his role as prophet. The ribbed garment is associated with priestly functions by the subject and inscription on the seal impression in Figure E, and by its similarity to the robe worn by the cross-bearer on 16*.

56*-60, with their long-robed Daniel , differ from 61-65*, with their kilted figure. The first group is characterized by deeper carving which results in rounded, well-defined forms. Modelling is preferred to the linear treatment of the second group. The figures of this latter group tend to be cursorily done, with portions of the figures left out entirely or sketchily shown. Such differences in execution may be due to varied workshop traditions; indeed, the costumes suggest regional distinction. If, on the basis of dress, 56*-60 can be associated with the Syriac-inscribed seal in Figure E, an origin in the Sasanian territories in northern Syria and Mesopotamia may be likely, while 61-65* may have been made in Iran. Yet 64 was found in Nippur, in southern Mesopotamia, and 16*, with its long-robed figure, may in fact have come from Bīshāpūr.

Since none of the seals is inscribed, they cannot be dated with any certainty, although on the basis of style, Lukonin assigns both 56* and 65* to the sixth or seventh century.[133] By analogy with Figure E, dated by Bivar to the fifth century, and with the Daniel of the seventh-eighth-century Byzantine bulla, 56*-60 may be placed in the latter half of the Sasanian period. Neither the shape nor material of the seals provides clues for provenance or dating. All are of the widespread bezel form, and are carnelian (56*, 62-65*), almandine (58*, 59 and 61) or amethyst (57* and 60): neither material is exclusive to one of the two groups.

The lions that threaten the kilted Daniel stand rampant on their hindlegs as do many of the beasts that oppose the oriental hero. Those that flank the long-robed Daniel always are inverted, with their heads on a level with his feet. This, too, is a traditional position for animal opponents, although their human adversary must grasp them by their hindlegs or tails, whereas Daniel does not touch them. Reversed lions are also standard in western - but, in particular, Byzantine - representations of Daniel.[134] In these, Daniel stands as an orant, while the lions make their obeisance by licking his feet. This detail is not part of the Biblical description, yet is found in many passions of the martyrs and corresponds to the oriental attitude of prostration which had been adopted by the Byzantine court.[135]

Contemporary with these images of Daniel are those of the Coptic Saint Menas, who appears on pilgrim flasks from Egypt as an orant between inverted camels.[136] If the Syro-Mesopotamian origin of the first group of Sasanian seals is correct, it then appears that the saint or prophet, flanked by obeisant animals, is an east Christian type that travelled north and west to influence Byzantine, North African,[137] and even Merovingian depictions of Daniel.[138]

V. Conclusion

The Christian attribution of seals 1*-30* has been possible through the recognition of obvious Christian motifs or of similar compositions in early Christian and Byzantine art. Seals 31*-65* with their Old Testament themes are, in my opinion, also Christian, although Jewish depictions of the Sacrifice of Isaac and Daniel in the Lions' Den must be considered. The placement of Isaac across the altar that characterizes the Sasanian seals (31*-52) finds its only known parallel in non-Sasanian art in the Synagogue at Dura-Europos. But this placement is not necessarily an exclusively Jewish trait nor the sole means of representation in Jewish art. In the only other definitely Jewish sacrifice scene, the sixth-century mosaic pavement in the Synagogue at Beth-Alpha, Abraham lifts Isaac into the air as if about to hurl him onto the flaming altar.[139] On an amulet in the Newell Collection, of presumable Jewish origin, Isaac walks towards the Hand of God which points to the ram standing beneath a small tree.[140] This second scene corresponds to many early Christian versions.[141]

That an eight-pointed star and not a cross appears above Isaac and the altar on the amulet should not be considered, as did Goodenough, proof of Jewish manufacture.[142] Neither cross nor star appears on some of the Sasanian seals, specifically on 31*, which, because of this omission, some have identified as Jewish.[143] The nearly identical scenes on 35, 36*-38*, 46, 48, 50* and 52 display a small cross with equal arms above the ram, and these seals certainly would have been owned by Christians and not by Jews.

The only attributably Jewish representation of Daniel in the Lions' Den occurs in a floor mosaic in the fifth-century synagogue at Na'aran (Ain Duk).[144] Although fragmentary, the scene can be reconstructed to show an orant Daniel between two standing lions. Some amulets with the scene have been accepted as Jewish representations but only because they are lacking the identifying cross.[145] There is no evidence that the scene was a Jewish invention, taken over by Christians; the episode appears in the catacombs as early as the third century. By analogy with

56*and 57* which display crosses, 58*-65* must be Christian.
That the Daniel motif - and also the Sacrifice of Isaac - was
shared as seal designs by both Jews and Christians, the latters'
ownership simply stated by the addition of a cross, is du-
bious.[146]

Actual Jewish pictorial models for the two scenes are as yet
unknown and perhaps were never developed. The existence of il-
luminated Hebrew Bibles does not seem to antedate the third
century, and Christian representations of both scenes are found
prior to the known Jewish ones.[147] Only the detail of Isaac upon the altar corresponds to an earlier, third-century Jewish
motif. The occurrence of this unique type on Sasanian seals
from as early as the fourth century on suggests some link with
the art of Dura, or, more likely, with that of a larger and
more influential center.[148] The Sacrifice scene in the Dura
Synagogue may be the only known survival of an iconographic
type that was extant in the Syro-Mesopotamian region. In the
complete absence of such monuments to show a more tangible
connection between Durene art and that in Sasanian territories
at a later time, this remains only a tantalizing possibility.

The choice by Sasanian Christians of the Sacrifice of Isaac and
Daniel in the Lions' Den may have had a significance beyond the
religious symbolism of both episodes. Their popularity as seal
designs, as shown by their number and the exclusion of other
Old Testament subjects, may not be fortuitous to this collection of seals. While liturgical considerations may have dicta-
ted their selection, resemblance of these two episodes to traditional oriental and Sasanian motifs must have also played a
part.[149] The hero between two lions and the worshipper before
an altar - or for the seals with orants, a worshipper alone -
are only demonstrably Christian by the addition of the cross.
By choosing one of these motifs, a Christian living in Persian
territory or a Persian convert would not have to call attention
to his belief, for fear of persecution, if he did not or could

not choose to do so, yet still satisfy himself with a meaning-
ful religious image for his personal signet.[150]

This does not imply that the New Testament scenes and seals
with crosses as their sole decoration always reflect a time or
region in which Christians were freer to call attention to themselves. The inscriptions on the seals that include the Zoroastrian formula and the Persian names of their owners attest to
the assimilation of Christians into Sasanian society. The
crosses with arms of equal length that appear in the field,
singly and in pairs, are within the tradition of Sasanian glyptic art besides having a special meaning to Persian Christians;
the embellishment of the cross with ribbons on 12*, 13 and 24*
is a uniquely Sasanian honorific device. The types and variety
of motifs on the Sasanian seals are notable in comparison with
that of the contemporary Christian West. The motifs of the Sasanian seals are shared with objects in other media that are
east Christian. Many of these are Syrian in origin, though possibly are of ultimate Constantinopolitan derivation.[151] The
strong influence of Egypt and Syria may be recognized in such
elements as dress, cross forms,[152] and the use of the cross
alone.[153] These have been adapted to the pervasive Sasanian
conventions of form and style.

Yet within our group, as with any collection of Sasanian seals
brought together according to subject matter, differences in
quality and style are noticeably apparent. Those of better quality, done in a "high" style that reflects such official monuments as the rock reliefs and coins, no doubt originated in the
royal or administrative centers of the empire (e.g. 24* and 55*).
The obvious differences in the manner of representation would
be temporal, and this is further indicated by the dating of the
associated inscriptions (supra, pp.8,19 and 21). Other seals,
such as 25*, 30*, 32* and 56*, are done in a manner that is
more typical of Sasanian glyptic art. Again, this should most
probably be seen as temporal: these examples are not earlier

than the fifth century, when the beginning of the widespread
use and manufacture of seals assured a greater chance for their
survival.[154] The more cursory or "stressed manner" of carving
appears to be characteristic of the last two centuries of the
Sasanian period, and this, in fact, is the style most prevalent
in our group.

Such differences, however, may in great part be geographical,
the result of diverse workshop traditions. If seals in the more
"official" mode were made in centers of Sasanian culture, those
of a more cursory rendering may be products of workshops in re-
mote or poor communities, as well as those that display a lack
of clarity in their particular choice of motif (28*, 30*, 44*).
Regional differences may be found in such features as clothing:
that of the long-robed cross-bearers and worshippers, and of
the first Daniel group, may be characteristic of Syro-Mesopotamian workshops.

Thus, the group of seals collected here reveals the existence
of diverse and localized Christian images and of localized
styles[155] throughout Syria, Mesopotamia and Iran in the early
centuries of Christianity.

CATALOGUE OF SEALS

The shapes of Sasanian seals are generally bezels, and ellipsoid
and hemispherical stamps. The bezels, to be set into metal
rings, are either oval or circular in shape, with straight or
bevelled sides. Unless otherwise noted, the sealing and the
back surfaces are flat. A variation of the bezel is the cabochon
which has an extremely convex face (11* and 21). The stamp
stamp seals included in this catalogue are perforated transver-
sely for suspension in a metal mount, and are either hemispherical or elliptical with slightly flattened sides; the back of
20* is carved with a geometric design. Another variation is a
stone ring which has a large perforation (22*). A full discussion of these shapes, with a suggested chronology for them, is
given by Bivar, pp. 20-24, with illustrations on pp. 142-45;
however, his conoid shape (p. 144) differs from that of 6*-9*.
The dimensions of the seals are provided when available in
millimeters; height or thickness precedes diameter or length
and width.

1. Pl. I, fig. 1. Leningrad, Hermitage, GL 830. Latin cross
   with expanding arms. Inscription No. 1. Chalcedony hemisphere: 9; 12. Borisov, op. cit., Pl. VI; Lukonin, No. 197.

2. Pl. I, fig. 2. Paris, Bibliothèque Nationale (formerly H.
   Seyrig Collection). Latin cross with expanding arms; encircled by dotted border and inscription No. 2. Carnelian bezel
   with convex face: 3; 11. Siegelkanon, No. 102a.

3. Pl. I, fig. 3. Paris, Bibliothèque Nationale (formerly H.
   Seyrig Collection). Latin cross above a globe, flanked by a
   crescent and a six-pointed star. Inscription No. 3. Carnelian
   bezel with convex face: 5; 22 x 20. Siegelkanon, 102a.

4. Berlin, VA 1587. Latin cross with bifurcated arms. Inscription No. 4. Carnelian bezel with convex face; dimensions not
   available. Horn and Steindorff, Pl. VI.

5. Tadjrish, Iran, S.Y. Nayeri Collection. Latin cross with bifurcated arms on an upright, rectangular stand. Inscription
   No. 5 along left side of cross. Chalcedony hemisphere; 33
   diameter. R.N. Frye, "Inscribed Seals from the Nayeri Collection", Forschungen zur Kunst Asiens: In Memoriam Kurt
   Erdmann (Istanbul, 1970), p. 23, No. 7 and fig. 13.

6. Pl. I, fig. 4. Paris, Bibliothèque Nationale (formerly H.
   Seyrig Collection). Latin cross with bifurcated dotted ends;
   a globe is between each forked extremity. The cross stands
   on a low platform. Syriac inscription to either side of the
   lower arm of the cross. Rock crystal conoid with slightly
   convex base: 21; 13 x 10.

7. Paris, Louvre D.284 (AOD 183; formerly M. Dieulafoy Collection). As 6*, with Syriac inscription. Rock crystal conoid:
   21; 13 x 11. Delaporte, Louvre I, Pl. 56:60; Survey IV,
   Pl. 256:QQ.

8. London, Southesk Collection. As 6*, Kufic inscription. Rock
   crystal conoid: 4. H. Carnegie (ed.), Catalogue of the Collection of Antique Gems formed by James Ninth Earl of
   Southesk, II (London, 1908), Pl. I: p. 29.

9. Pl. I, fig. 5. Paris, Bibliothèque Nationale (formerly H.
   Seyrig Collection). Latin cross with bifurcated ends; a
   globe between each fork. Kufic inscription. Rock crystal
   conoid with slightly convex base: 22; 13 x 12.

10. Calcutta, Indian Museum 8239. Latin cross as on 6*; enclosed
    by a wreath border. Kufic inscription. Rock crystal; shape
    and dimensions not available.

11. Pl. I, fig. 6. London WA 120260. As 6*; the cross stands
    upon a vertical base that is supported by a small globe.
    Inscription No. 6. Chalcedony cabochon: 10 x 11. Thomas,
    loc. cit. (supra, n. 9); Bivar, Pl. 27: NA 1; Siegelkanon,
    102a.

12. Pl. I, fig. 7. Paris, Louvre D,283 (AOD 172; formerly M.
    Dieulafoy Collection). Latin cross with perpendicular ter-
    minations; flanked by two dots above cross arm, upturned
    ribbons tied to the lowest extremity; enclosed by an arch.
    Ruby bezel with convex face: 2; 11 x 10. Delaporte, Louvre
    I, Pl. 56-58; Siegelkanon, 102a.

13. Berlin, VA 1603. Cross with arms of equal length and per-
    pendicular terminations; horizontal bar above and upturned
    ribbons (?) below. Garnet bezel with convex face; dimen-
    sions not available. Horn and Steindorff, Pl. VI; Siegel-
    kanon, 102a.

14. Pl. I, fig. 8. Paris, Bibliothèque Nationale (formerly H.
    Seyrig Collection). Two horizontal lines of a Syriac
    inscription between small crosses. Chalcedony hemisphere:
    14; 17.

15. Pl. I, fig. 9. London, British Museum, Dept. of Medieval
    and Later Antiquities 89, 10-14, 1 (formerly Greville
    Chester Collection). Two angels holding a wreath between
    them above a Latin cross. Below, inscription No. 7.
    Carnelian hemisphere: 5 diameter. Dalton, Catalogue, No. 82
    (not illustrated); idem, Engraved Gems, Pl. XVIII:547.

16. Pl. II, fig. 10. London WA 103003. Long-robed male figure
    standing to the right holding a cross-shaped staff.
    Inscription No. 8. Agate ellipsoid: 15 x 20. Bivar, Pl. 5:
    BE 2.

17. Pl. II, fig. 11. Leningrad, Hermitage GL 193. Long-robed male

figure standing to the right holding a cross-shaped staff;
a small cross with arms of equal length to the left, behind
him. Garnet bezel: 2; 11 x 9. Borisov, op. cit., Pl.VI;
Lukonin, No. 161 (not illustrated).

18. Pl.II, fig.12. Teheran, M. Foroughi Collection. Long-robed
figure standing to the right holding a cross-shaped staff.
Inscription No. 9. Chalcedony hemisphere: 8; 12.

19. Pl.II, fig.13. London WA 119396; possibly from Warka
(purchased, 1928). Figure standing to the right holding a
cross (?). Carnelian dome: 9 diameter. Bivar, Pl. 5: BE 3.

20. Pl.II, fig.14. Teheran, M. Foroughi Collection. Long-robed
male figure standing to the right, in prayer; a cross with
equal arms is before him, another is behind, above an altar.
Chalcedony ellipsoid with decorated back: 22; 21 x 16.

21. Philadelphia, University Museum (formerly M. Sommerville
Collection). Long-robed male figure standing to the right
in prayer; two crosses with arms of equal length to either
side. Garnet cabochon; dimensions not available.
M. Sommerville, Engraved Gems. Their History and an Elaborate View of Their Place in Art (Philadelphia, 1889, Pl.
75: 945 (identified as a Christian gem, p. 730); C.C. Ver-
meule, Cameo and Intaglio. Engraved Gems from the Sommerville Collection (The University Museum, Philadelphia,
30 November 1956-31 March 1957) No. 33 (not illustrated).

22. Pl.II, fig.15. Berlin, Museum für Islamische Kunst, VA 1075.
Male figure in orant posture; a cross with arms of equal
length to either side. Inscription No. 10. Chalcedony stone
ring (fragment): 17 x 11. Horn and Steindorff, Pl. I.

23. Pl.III, fig.16. Tadjrish, Iran, S.Y. Nayeri Collection. Male
orant; two crosses with arms of equal length to either side.
Inscription No. 11. Chalcedony; bezel: 17 x 14. Frye,
"Inscribed Seals from the Nayeri Collection", p. 21, No. 1

and fig. 7.

24. Pl.III, fig.17. Paris, Bibliothèque Nationale, 1331a. Busts
    of a man and a woman facing each other with their inner
    arms raised towards a ribboned cross above and between
    them; an unribboned cross is below; the man holds a cross(?)
    in his raised hand. Surrounding them is inscription No. 12.
    Nicolo bezel set in a modern gold ring: 15 x 12. Smirnov,
    op. cit., fig. 1; Babelon, Guide illustré, No. 1400[c] (not
    illustrated); Siegelkanon, 17a.

25. Pl.III, fig.18. Paris, Bibliothèque Nationale, 1332. Two
    female figures facing each other, joining hands; a cross
    with arms of equal length, a star and a crescent are be-
    tween them. Inscription No. 13. Carnelian bezel: 3;
    16 x 13. Chabouillet, op. cit., p. 191 (not illustrated);
    Babelon, Guide illustré, No. 1400[d] (fig. 22); Ghirshman,
    Persian Art, fig. 294[e]; Siegelkanon, 12c.

26. Pl.III, fig.19. New York, Metropolitan Museum of Art, Dept.
    of Ancient Near Eastern Art 81.6.287 (formerly C.W. King
    Collection). Two female figures facing each other; between
    them a cross. Carnelian bezel: 3; 17 x 15. King, The
    Gnostics, No. 18 (facing p. 108); idem, Antique Gems and
    Rings, II, Pl. IV:13; Von der Osten, "The Ancient Seals
    from the Near East", fig. 111.

27. Pl.III, fig.20. Teheran, M. Foroughi Collection. Two female
    figures facing each other; a crescent and a cross between
    them. Carnelian bezel: 3; 19 x 14.

28. Pl.III, fig.21. Paris, Bibliothèque Nationale 1331. Female
    figure seated to the right, with a child on her lap. Be-
    hind, to the left, inscription No. 14. Garnet bezel with
    convex face: 4; 12 x 10. Chabouillet, op. cit., p. 191
    (not illustrated); Garrucci, op. cit., VI. Pl. 497; 18;
    Siegelkanon, 12 b.

29. Pl. IV, fig. 22. Teheran, M. Foroughi Collection. Male figure facing right, mounted on a donkey or an ass, flanked by groups of three figures; a cross with arms of equal length appear on either side and above each group which appears to be held by one of the figures in the left-hand group. Chalcedony ellipsoid: 23; 21 x 18.

30. Pl. IV, fig. 23. Cambridge, Massachusetts, Harvard Semitic Museum. Male figure facing right, mounted on an ass and holding a cross with arms of equal length; a six-pointed star is in front of the animal. Inscription No. 15. Banded agate disk: 10; 21 diameter.

31. Pl. IV, fig. 24. Paris, Bibliothèque Nationale 1330. Bearded male figure to the right, a knife in his raised hand, standing before an altar upon which lies the figure of a child. Behind, to the left, a ram is behind a bush. The bearded figure turns his head to the left to look at a hand in the sky, above the ram. Banded agate bezel: 3; 20 diameter. Chabouillet, op. cit., p. 191 (not illustrated); Garrucci, op. cit., VI, Pl. 497:9; Babelon, Guide illustré, No. 1400[a] (not illustrated); Bonner, op. cit., Pl. XIX:344; Siegelkanon, 4d.

32. Pl. IV, fig. 25. Paris, Bibliothèque Nationale 1330a/N.4798. Bearded male figure stands as in 31*, but to the left, before an altar upon which reclines a small stick-figure, and turns his head to the right towards a ram standing before a small tree. Above, inscription No. 16. Carnelian bezel with convex back: 4; 18 x 12. Siegelkanon, 4c.

33. Pl. IV, fig. 26. Leningrad, Hermitage GL 1402. As 32*; the ram stands on a groundline. No inscription. Carnelian bezel: 2; 18 x 13.

34. Chicago, Oriental Institute A,2484. As 32*, but a large tree is between the bearded figure and the ram and there is

no inscription. Carnelian bezel: 20 x 14. M.F. Williams,
"The Collection of Western Asiatic Seals in the Haskell
Oriental Museum (Oriental Institute)", American Journal of
Semitic Languages, XLIV (1928), No. 93.

35. Leningrad, Hermitage GL 326. Bearded male figure to
    right, a knife in his raised hand, standing before an
    altar. He turns his head to the left towards the figure of
    a ram, and behind it, a bush. Above the ram's head is a
    cross with arms of equal length. Carnelian bezel: 4;
    14 x 11. Borisov, op. cit., Pl. VI:3; Lukonin, No. 154.

36. Pl. IV, fig. 27. Oxford, Ashmolean Museum, 1961. 534. As 35,
    but the bearded figure looks towards the altar, the bush is
    omitted and the cross appears above the ram's hindquarters.
    Nicolo bezel: 3; 14 x 12.

37. Pl. IV, fig. 28. Vienna, Kunsthistorisches Museum, X 109. As
    35, but without the bush and a cross with arms of equal
    length above the ram's hindquarters. Carnelian ellipsoid:
    15; 15 x 11.

38. Pl. IV, fig. 29. Leningrad, Hermitage GL 841. As 37*. Carne-
    lian bezel: 3; 19 x 13. Lukonin, No. 158 (not illustrated).

39. Leningrad, Hermitage GL 1249. As 37*, but without the cross
    above the ram. Carnelian bezel: 3; 13 x 12. Lukonin, No.156.

40. Leningrad, Hermitage GL 825. As 39. Carnelian bezel: 3;
    12 x 9. Lukonin, No. 157 (not illustrated).

41. Berlin VA 1080. As 39. Carnelian bezel; dimensions not
    available. Horn and Steindorff, Pl. I.

42. Pl. V, fig. 30. London OA 5. As 39 but oriented to the left;
    the ram stands on a groundline. Carnelian bezel: 13 x 11.
    Bivar, Pl. 5: BD 16; Siegelkanon, 4c.

43. Tiflis, Georgian State Museum 65N. From a grave at Mtskhet-
    Samtavro. Male figure stands to the right, facing an altar,
    a knife in one hand. Behind him is a ram. Carnelian bezel
    in a bronze ring: 13 x 10. Makhsimova, op. cit., Pl. III:
    83.

44. Pl. V, fig. 31. London WA 119616. Bearded male figure
    standing to the left before an altar and looking behind
    him, to the right. Carnelian bezel in a silver ring:
    9 x 13. Bivar, Pl. 5:BD 5; Siegelkanon, 4c

45. Pl. V, fig. 32. Toronto, Royal Ontario Museum D. 1554. As
    43. Carnelian bezel with a highly convex face: 4; 18 x 12.
    T.J. Meek, "Ancient Oriental Seals in the Royal Ontario
    Museum", Berytus, VIII (1943), Pls. IV: 48 and VI.

46. London WA 119837. As 37*; the scene is encircled by a
    wreath. Almandine bezel: 11 x 9. Bivar, Pl. 8:CG 3.

47. Berlin VA 1078. As 46, without the cross above the ram.
    Agate hemisphere; dimensions not available. Horn and Stein-
    dorff, Pl. I.

48. Berlin VA 1079. As 37*. Agate ellipsoid; dimensions not
    available. Horn and Steindorff, Pl. I; Siegelkanon, 4 c.

49. Pl. V, fig. 33. Leningrad, Hermitage GL 256. As 39 but the
    figure upon the altar is omitted. Hematite ellipsoid: 12;
    15 x 13. Lukonin, No. 155 (not illustrated).

50. Pl. V, fig. 34. Vienna, Kunsthistorisches Museum, IX 1648.
    As 38*, but the altar is omitted. Hematite ellipsoid: 16;
    17 x 13.

51. Paris, Louvre A.1437 (AO 7189). As 49*. Hematite ellipsoid:
    20; 20 x 13. Delaporte, Louvre II, Pl. 111:24^{b}.

52. Paris, Louvre A.1442 (AO 6136). As 38*. Hematite ellipsoid:

16; 17 x 12. Delaporte, Louvre II, Pl. 111:25.

53. Oxford, Ashmolean Museum 1922.63. As 52. Hematite hemisphere: 9; 15 diameter.

54. New York, Metropolitan Museum of Art. Department of Ancient
Near Eastern Art 93.22.64. As 37*. Hematite hemisphere: 10;
19 diameter. Von der Osten, "The Ancient Seals from the
Near East", fig. 28.

55. Pl. V, fig.35. Boston, Museum of Fine Arts, Department of
Egyptian and Near Eastern Art, 65.1649 (formerly, Moussa
Collection, Teheran). Bearded male figure moving to the
right, a knife in his hand, towards a small male figure
that is seated upon a rocky knoll; the group is placed on
a groundline. Behind, is a ram, to the right. Above, inscription No. 17. Carnelian bezel with convex face: 3;
14 x 10.

56. Pl.VI, fig.36. Leningrad, Hermitage GL 838. Male figure in
a long robe stands with frontal body and head in right
profile and holds a cross in his two raised hands. To
either sind is a lion with its head downwards. Carnelian
bezel with slightly convex face; 2; 12 diameter. Lukonin,
No. 189 (listed as GL 933); Segal, op. cit., Pl. IV:c

57. Pl.VI, fig.37. Leningrad, Hermitage GL 933. As 56*, but the
crosses are in the field between the figure's hands and
head. Amethyst bezel: 3; 13 diameter.

58. Pl.VI, fig.38. London WA 119821. As 56*, without the
crosses. Almandine bezel: 12 x 13. Smirnov, op. cit., fig.
12; Segal, op. cit., Pl. IV:b; Bivar, Pl. 8:CG 8; Siegelkanon, 2d.

59. New York, Metropolitan Museum of Art, Department of Ancient
Near Eastern Art 81.6.276 (formerly C.W. King Collection).
As 58*. Almandine bezel: 1; 9x 11. H.H. Von der Osten, "The

Museum Collection of Oriental Seal-Stones", _Bulletin of the Metropolitan Museum of Art_, XX (1925), fig. 5, p. 83, _idem_, "The Ancient Seals from the Near East", fig. 107.

60. Oxford, Ashmolean Museum 1968. 1217 (EF 79; formerly Greville J. Chester Collection). As _56_; scene encircled by a wreath. Amethyst bezel; 2; 12 diameter. C.D.E. Fortnum, "Additional Notes on Finger Rings and on Some Engraved Gems of the Early Christian Period", _The Archaeological Journal_, XXXVII (1880), p. 362, no. 11.

61. Tiflis, Georgian State Museum 18046. From the excavations at Mtskheta-Samtavro. Male figure in a knee-length kilt stands, with his body in frontal view and his head in right profile, and his arms raised, between two rampant lions. Almandine bezel: 10 x 13. A.A. Zakharov, "Gemmen und Siegel des Museums Georgiens", _Vestnik Muzeja Gruzii_, V (1930), Pl. I:25.

62. Tiflis, Georgian State Museum 60-12/5. As _61_. Carnelian bezel: 10 diameter. _Ibid._, Pl. I:16.

63. Leningrad, Hermitage GL 74. As 61. Carnelian bezel: 12 x 10. Lukonin, No. 188.

64. Philadelphia, University Museum CBS 9403. As _61_. Carnelian bezel: 1; 12 diameter. Legrain, _op. cit._, Pl. XXXV:738.

65. Pl.VI, fig.39. Leningrad, Hermitage GL 1385. Bearded male figure in a knee-length kilt stands with frontal body, his head in right profile, and his hands clasped at his waist. To either side is a rampant lion, touching a small dot or globe with its forepaws. Carnelian bezel: 2; 11 x 9.

APPENDIX

THE PAHLAVI INSCRIPTIONS ON THE SEALS

Richard N. Frye

No. 1 (Seal <u>1</u>*) ᵓwxrmzd gwšnp'
"Ohrmazd-Gušnasp"

No. 2 (Seal <u>2</u>*) mᵓnybwč ŠM
"Maniboz (is my) name"

No. 3 (Seal <u>3</u>*) Two different scripts (right and left). The
right side makes no sense: ᵓtlykwny; pro-
bably and attempt to copy an earlier (fifth
century) script by an illiterate carver. The
left side does not seem to mean anything,
but is a copy of a later (seventh century)
script: ᵓlšn w blᵓnyk'

No. 4 (Seal <u>4</u>) bwrzp' or bn'pš
proper name, although the reading is doubt-
ful.

No. 5 (Seal <u>5</u>) bᵓmwrdt (?)
proper name.

No. 6 (Seal <u>11</u>*) pᵓky
"pure"

No. 7 (Seal <u>15</u>*) ᵓpnᵓm gblwn'
proper name?

No. 8 (Seal <u>16</u>*) bᵓnᵓwḥy šbg...
proper name?

No. 9 (Seal <u>18</u>*) yᵓn bᵓḥy šbyn (?)

No. 10 (Seal <u>22</u>*) mwšt ᵓpstᵓn ⁶L yzdᵓn
"Mavišt, refuge in (the) God(s)"

No. 11 (Seal <u>23</u>*) yzdᵓndᵓt ᵓpstᵓn ⁶L yzdᵓn
"Yazdāndāt, refuge in (the) God(s)"

No. 12 (Seal <u>24</u>*) ᵓpdḥpy...sᵓn ᵓpstᵓn (⁶L) yz(dt)y
"(proper name), refuge in God"

No. 13 (Seal <u>25</u>*) ᵓpstᵓn ⁶L yzdᵓn
"Refuge in (the) God(s)"

No. 14 (Seal <u>28</u>*) (bš) bwst'
proper name?

No. 15 (Seal <u>30</u>*) ᵓpstᵓn ⁶L yz...
"Refuge in (the) God(s)"

No. 16 (Seal <u>32</u>*)   <u>mtryny</u>
                             "Mihrēn"

No. 17 (Seal <u>55</u>*)   <u>ZNH</u> <u>mwdly</u> <u>l'(st)</u>
                             "This seal is valid"

INDEX OF PROPER NAMES

ABBREVIATIONS

Berlin VA   Islamisches Museum, East Berlin, for seals with designation, unless otherwise noted as Museum für Islamische Kunst, West Berlin

Bivar   A.D.H. Bivar, Catalogue of the Western Asiatic Seals in the British Museum, Stamp Seals, II: The Sassanian Dynasty (London, 1969).

DACL   F. Cabrol and H. LeClercq, Dictionnaire d'archéologie chrétienne et de liturgie (Paris, 1907-53).

Dalton, BAA   O.M. Dalton, Byzantine Art and Archaeology (Oxford, 1911).

Dalton, Catalogue   O.M. Dalton, Catalogue of Early Christian Antiquities and Objects from the Christian East ... in the British Museum (London, 1901)

Dalton, Engraved Gems   O.M. Dalton, Catalogue of the Engraved Gems of the Post-Classical Periods in the Department of British and Mediaeval Antiquities and Ethnography in the British Museum (London, 1915).

Dalton, Guide   O.M. Dalton, A Guide to the Early Christian and Byzantine Antiquities in the Department of British and Mediaeval Antiquities, The British Museum (London, 1903).

Delaporte, Louvre I, II   L. Delaporte, Catalogue des cy-

lindres, cachets et pierres gravées de style orientale, Musée du
Louvre, I-II (Paris, 1920-23).

DOC I-III   M.C. Ross, Catalogue of the By-
zantine and Early Mediaeval An-
tiquities in the Dumbarton Oaks
Collection, I-II (Washington,
D.C., 1962-65); K. Weitzmann, III
(Washington, D.C., 1972).

Grabar, Ampoules   A. Grabar, Ampoules de Terre
Sainte (Paris, 1958).

Grabar, Iconography   A. Grabar, Christian Iconography.
A Study of Its Origins ("Bollingen
Series", XXXV,10, Princeton,
1968).

Horn and Steindorff   P. Horn and G. Steindorff, Sasanidische Siegelsteine ("König-
liche Museen zu Berlin, Mitteilungen aus den orientalischen
Sammlungen", IV [1891]).

Lexikon   E. Kirschbaum (ed.), Lexikon der
christlichen Ikonographie, I-II
(Rome, Freiburg, Basel, Vienna,
1968-70).

London OA   London, British Museum, Department of Oriental Antiquities.

London WA   London, British Museum, Department of Western Asiatic Antiqui-
ties.

Lukonin   A.Ja. Borisov and V.G. Lukonin,
Sasanidskie gemmy. Katalog sobra-
niya gosudarstvennogo ermitazha

(Leningrad, 1963).

Siegelkanon   R. Göbl, Der Sāsānidische Siegel-
               kanon ("Handbücher der Mittel-
               asiatischen Numismatik", IV,
               Braunschweig, 1973).

Survey   A.U. Pope (ed.), A Survey of
               Persian Art from Prehistoric
               Times to the Present (Oxford,
               1938-39).

NOTES

* The seals discussed here are referred to by their catalogue
number which I have assigned according to the order of their
discussion. Those with numbers that are asterisked are illustrated in the plates. The description of each seal's
design is based upon its impression.

1. Some general sources are J. Labourt, Le Christianisme dans
l'Empire sous la dynastie sassanide (2nd ed., Paris, 1904);
A. Christensen, L'Iran sous les Sassanides (2nd ed., rev.,
Copenhagen, 1944), pp. 487-92; M.-L. Chaumont, "Les Sassanides et la christianisation de l'Empire iranien au IIIe
siècle de notre ère", Revue de l'histoire des religions,
CLXV (1964), pp. 165-202; J.-P. Asmussen, "Das Christentum
in Iran und sein Verhältnis zum Zoroastrismus", Studia
Theologica, XVI (1962), pp. 1-22; also G. Downey, A History
of Antioch in Syria from Seleucus to the Arab Conquest,
(Princeton, 1961), pp. 259-61, 309; J.M. Fiey, "Topographie
chrétienne de Mahozé", L'Orient syrien, XII (1967), pp. 397-
420; R. Ghirshman, Persian Art: the Parthian and Sassanian
Dynasties, 249 B.C.-A.D. 651 (trans. S. Gilbert and J.
Emmons, New York, 1962), pp. 287-89; E. Herzfeld, Archaeological History of Iran (London, 1934), pp. 103-04; G.
Pigulevskaya, Les Villes de l'état iranien aux époques
parthe et sassanide. Contributions à l'histoire sociale de
la Basse Antiquité (Paris, Mouton, The Hague, 1963), pp.161-
75, 186, 244-51.

2. Ctesiphon: E. Meyer, "Seleukia und Ktesiphon", Mitteilungen
der Deutschen Orient Gesellschaft, 67 (April, 1929), pp. 23-
5; O. Reuther, "The German Excavations at Ctesiphon",
Antiquity, III (1929), pp. 449-51.
Hīra: D. Talbot Rice, "The Oxford Excavations at Hīra,1931",
Antiquity, VI (1932), pp. 276-91; idem, "Hīra", Journal of
the Royal Central Asian Society, XIX (1932), pp. 254-68;

idem, "The Oxford Excavations at Hīra", <u>Ars Islamica</u>, I
(1934), pp. 51-73.
For a general discussion of the architectural remains at
these sites and others, see K. Erdmann, <u>Die Kunst Irans zur
Zeit der Sasaniden</u> (Berlin, 1943), pp. 43-44 and O. Reuther,
<u>Survey</u> I, pp. 560-61

3. Herzfeld, <u>op</u>. <u>cit</u>., pp. 103-4 and Pls. XVIII-XIX; Ghirshman,
   <u>op</u>. <u>cit</u>., p. 278 and <u>idem</u>, <u>The Island of Khārg</u> (Teheran,
   1960); J. Bowman, "The Sasanian Church in the Khārg Island",
   <u>Acta Iranica III</u>: Commémoration Cyrus II: Hommage Universel,
   (Téhéran-Liège, 1974), pp. 217-20.

4. C. Wilkinson, "Christian Remains from Nīshāpūr", <u>Forschungen
   zur Kunst Asiens: In Memoriam Kurt Erdmann</u> (Istanbul, 1970),
   pp. 79-87. Further east, a Christian church has been found
   at Merv in Turkmenistan (G.A. Pugachenkova, <u>Iskusstvo Turk-
   menistana</u> [Mosvow, 1967], pp. 86-7 with plan).

5. A. Chabouillet, <u>Catalogue général et raisonné des camées et
   pierres gravées de la Bibliothèque Nationale</u> (Paris, 1858),
   p. 191. His Nos. 1330-1332 are our <u>31</u>*, <u>28</u>*, and <u>25</u>*,
   respectively.

6. C.W. King, <u>The Gnostics and Their Remains</u> (London, 1864),
   pp. 143-44; <u>Antique Gems and Rings</u> (London, 1872), I, p. 84
   and II, pp. 28-30.

7. Ja.I. Smirnov, <u>Serebranjanoe sirijskoe bljudo najdennoe v'
   Permskom' Krae</u> ("Materialy po arkheologii Rossii", 22, St.
   Petersburg, 1899), p. 36.

8. D. Osborne, <u>Engraved Gems: Signets, Talismans and Ornamental
   Intaglios, Ancient and Modern</u> (New York, 1912), pp. 151-52.

9. E. Thomas, "Notes Introductory to Sassanian Mint Monograms
   and Gems. With a Supplementary Notice on the Arabico-Pehlvi
   Series of Persian Coins", <u>Journal of the Royal Asiatic So-
   ciety</u>, XIII (1852), p. 425, No. 71 and Pl. III (shown upside
   down).

10. A.Ja. Barisov, "Epigraficheskie Zametki, III: Ob odnoj
    gruppe sasanidskikh reznykh kamnej", Trudy otdela vostoka
    Gosudarstvennogo Ermitazha, I (1939), pp. 235-42;
    P. Ackerman briefly discussed Christian seals in Survey I,
    p. 811.

11. Bivar, pp. 28-9.
    The most recent discussion of Christian - and Jewish - seals
    of the Sasanian period is that of S. Shaked, who considers
    whether seals with single or multiple crosses are attribut-
    able to Christian owners. "Jewish and Christian Seals of
    the Sasanian Period", Gaston Wiet Memorial Volume (Jerusa-
    lem, forthcoming). I am grateful to Dr. Shaked for allowing
    me to read his article in typescript.

12. 1*, so dated by Lukonin, p. 108 (inscription No. 36, on p.
    53) and Frye; the inscription on 2* is dated by Frye (see
    appendix).

13. Survey, Pl. 1442C (from Rayy); G.A. Eisen and F. Kouchakji,
    Glass, Its Origin, History, Chronology, Technique and Clas-
    sification to the Sixteenth Century, II (New York, 1927),
    figs. 198 and 200 and Pl. 121, left; Masterpieces of Glass
    (Exhibition Catalogue, The British Museum, London, 1968),
    No. 80 (from Aleppo). The flasks traditionally are dated to
    the fourth to sixth centuries. Recently D. Barag dated the
    group with Christian motifs - and by analogy, those with
    Jewish ones - to the period between 578 and 636 because of
    the appearance of the stepped cross ("Glass Pilgrim Vessels
    from Jerusalem, Part I", Journal of Glass Studies, XII
    [1970], pp. 44-6; supra, p. 4). Those vessels showing the
    cross without the steps and with expanding arms, however,
    could be earlier since the hexagonal shape, according to
    Barag, seems to have been popular as early as the fifth
    century ("Glass Pilgrim Vessels from Jerusalem, Parts II
    and III", Journal of Glass Studies, XIII [1971], p. 57).

14. Sasanian Silver, Late Antique and Early Medieval Arts of

Luxury from Iran (The University of Michigan Museum of Art, Ann Arbor, 1967), No. 53, p. 135.

15. O. Grabar, in ibid., p. 42.

16. A. Grabar, Martyrium; Recherches sur les Cults des Reliques et l'art chrétien antique, II (Paris, 1946), pp. 275-76; C. Nordenfalk, "An Illustrated Diatessaron", The Art Bulletin, L (1968), p. 123 with bibliography on the triumphal cross on the stepped platform in n. 23. For a contrary interpretation of the motif as a sign of Christianity triumphing over Persian paganism, see K. Ericsson, "The Cross on Steps and the Silver Hexagram", Jahrbuch der Österreichischen Byzantinischen Gesellschaft, XVII (1968), p. 149ff.

17. W. Wroth, Imperial Byzantine Coins in the British Museum (2 vols. in one, reprint of the 1908 ed., Chicago, 1966), p. lxxxvi and Pl. XVI:16 and 18. P. Grierson, Catalogue of the Byzantine Coins in the Dumbarton Oaks Collection and in the Whittemore Collection, II: Phocas to Theodosius III (602-717), Part I: Phocas and Heraclius (602-641), (Washington, D.C., 1968), pp. 95-96.

18. Wroth, op. cit., Pl. XXIII:2-12

19. Grabar, Ampoules, Pls. XXIII and XXV; XLI: Monza, Nos. 12 and 13; Bobbio, No. 8.

20. D.V. Ainalov, The Hellenistic Origins of Byzantine Art (trans. E.& S. Sobelvitch; ed. C. Mango, New Brunswick, N.J., 1961), fig. 116.

21. Ibid., fig. 119 and Smirnov's monograph (supra, n. 7).

22. Ainalov, op. cit., pp. 75 and 262

23. Grabar, Ampoules, Pl. XI, 1

24. R. Göbl, Sasanian Numismatics (trans. P. Severin, Braunschweig, 1971), Table XII and Pl. 14:222 (coinage of Khusrō II), and p. 21.

25. Beginning with Perōz (459-484), the coin reverses show a six- or eight-pointed star and a horizontal crescent, usually to the left and right, respectively, of the flames of the fire altar (loc. cit., and Pl. 10: 167ff). The star and crescent will often flank portrait busts on the seals (Bivar, Pl. 3: AD 1, AE 8, AF 4,6 and 8). Crescents and stars, either separately or together, are common devices on the seals.

26. Grabar, Ampoules, Pl. X,2.

27. Eisen and Kouchakji, op. cit., p. 490, fig. 205, DOC I, No. 97 (Pl. LII:B). Eisen and Kouckakji date them to the fourth century, but Ross's sixth-century attribution seems more convincing (pp. 82-3).

28. Wilkinson, op. cit., fig. 5 (now in the Bezalel Museum, Jerusalem).

29. Ibid., figs. 1, 2 and 4 (inkwell and dish in the Metropolitan Museum of Art and bowl in the Iran Bastan Museum, Teheran, all from Nīshāpūr).

30. Ibid., fig. 1.

31. G. Gropp, "Die Pahlavi-Inschrift aus dem Thomaskreuz in Madras", Archäologische Mitteilungen aus Iran, N.F. III (1970), p. 270, fig. 2; B.T. Anklesaria, "The Pahlavi Inscription on the Crosses in Southern India", Journal of the Cama Oriental Society, XCIII (1958), p. 63. Gropp also illustrates a trefoliated cross on a doorpost from the royal city of Anuradhapura, Ceylon (fig. 2), dated to the Portuguese period. He notes that according to The Christian Topography of Cosmas Indicopleustes, Persian Christians were in the city as early as the sixth century (p. 271).

32. H. Stern, "Les Représentations des conciles dans l'Eglise de la Nativité à Bethléhem", Byzantion, XI (1936), pp. 149-151. Stern postulates a Palestinian origin for this type of cross and interprets it as the Living Cross.

33. Grabar, Ampoules, Pl. XXXII: fragment 1: the cross is enclosed by a mandorla and is set upon the rocky ground of Golgotha.

34. Rice, Antiquity, VI, fig. 3d; splayed arms ending in dots without the central globe also occur (figs. 3f and 4a and b).

35. Stern, op. cit., Pl. XIV, 39.

36. Rice, Ars Islamica, I, p. 56, fig. 7.

37. Conical stamp seals appear among the Assyrian seals about 700 B.C., and continue into Neo-Babylonian and Achaemenid times (sixth-third centuries B.C.). See H.H. Von der Osten, Ancient Oriental Seals in the Collection of Mr. Edward T. Newell ("Oriental Institute Publications", XXII, Chicago, 1934), fig. 2: Nos. 484, 498, 517, 624, and p. 9. A survival of a conical stamp seal into Seleucid or even Parthian times is ibid., Pl. XXXV:626.

38. For example, a seal with a cock on an altar in Survey IV, Pl. 255:T = L. Legrain, The Culture of the Babylonians from Their Seals in the Collections of the University Museum (Philadelphia, 1923), Pl. XLVIII:1047.

39. D. Talbot Rice, "The Leaved Cross", Byzantinoslavica, XI (1950), pp. 72ff. A cross with splayed ends decorates a capital in the Archaeological Museum, Istanbul, that is dated to the time of Justinian, the middle of the sixth century. It sprouts from the tips of its upright arm an elaborate leafy design (M. Usman, "Sur quelques chapiteaux byzantines", Actes du Xe Congrès international d'études byzantines, Istanbul, 15-21, IX, 1955 [Istanbul, 1957], Pl. XXXVIII:7). A leaved cross also decorates a side of the hexagonal glass cruet in the Dumbarton Oaks Collection (supra, n. 27).

40. Rice, Antiquity, VI, fig. 4a and b.

41. Wilkinson, op. cit., fig. 8.

42. Rice, "The Leaved Cross", p. 74 and Gropp, op. cit., p. 269
    for the Italian evidence; W. Kleiss, "Bericht über zwei Er-
    kundungsfahrten in Nordwest-Iran", Archäologische Mittei-
    lungen aus Iran, N.F. II (1962), p. 122, fig. 124 and Pl.
    51,3 for Armenian examples; and Rice, "The Leaved Cross",
    pp. 72-3 for Byzantine examples.

43. Ampoules, p. 60. Yet Grabar notes that it is appropriate to
    the iconography of the ampullae which were important equip-
    ment in the cult of the Palestinian holy places, specific-
    ally Golgotha, as containers for the oil which was blessed
    during ceremonies associated with the relic of the True
    Cross.

44. For example, Wroth, op. cit., Pl. VI:16. Crosses with arms
    of equal length and perpendicular terminations are placed
    in the field among twelve figures (Apostles?) who worship a
    large Latin cross on an intaglio in Munich (A. Furtwängler,
    Die antiken Gemmen, I [Leipzig, 1900], Pl. LXVII:6).

45. The idea of glorification by two attending Victories was
    taken over from the West by the Sasanians for the late sixth
    early seventh-century relief at Tāq-i Būstān where two
    diadem-bearing Victories appear in the spandrels of the
    large iwan arch to frame the royal investiture scene within
    (A. Godard, The Art of Iran, trans. M. Heron; ed. M. Rogers
    [New York and Washington, D.C., 1965], Pl. 113).

46. British Museum, Department of Medieval and Later Antiqui-
    ties 67, 7-19, 3 (Dalton, Engraved Gems, Pl. XVIII:517 and
    idem, Catalogue, No. 17).

47. K. Wessel, Koptische Kunst, Die Spätantike in Ägypten
    (Recklinghausen, 1963), fig. X.

48. Bivar suggests that the seal could be interpreted as "that
    of a Christian bishop of Bīshāpūr" (p. 28). However, for
    Frye's reading, see Appendix, No. 8.

49. R.N. Frye, The Heritage of Persia (Cleveland and New York, 1963), p. 204.

50. J. Beckwith, The Art of Constantinople. An Introduction to Byzantine Art, 330-1453 (London and New York, 1968), fig. 12; H. Goodacre, A Handbook of the Coinage of the Byzantine Empire (London, 1957), pp. 33 and 37ff for the coinage of Theodosius' successors.

51. A.A. Vasiliev, Justin the First (Cambridge, Mass., 1950), p. 422; See DOC II, No. 63 (late sixth-century gold intaglio of an Archangel-Victory with the cross-shaped staff and globe).

52. Dalton, Engraved Gems, Nos. 550-553 and a pottery stamp of the sixth century (Dalton, BAA, fig. 387: the figure is identified as the Archangel Michael); DOC I, No. 117 (also identified by its Greek inscription as the Archangel Michael).

53. Bivar, Pl. 5: BD 1-4, 6 and &. The gesture of a raised hand, usually with palm facing away from the person, is known in Iran since Achaemenid times (and earlier in the Near East) as a sign of reverence before a deity (R.N. Frye, "Gestures of Deference to Royalty in Ancient Iran", Iranica Antiqua, IX [1972], pp. 103-04.

54. C. Bonner, Studies in Magical Amulets (Ann Arbor, 1950), Pl. XVIII:334 (in the British Museum).

55. Ibid., p. 223 and citation of figs. 119-120 in Dalton, BAA.

56. Bivar, Pl. 5: BD 2.

57. Ibid., Pl. 27: NA 2: A.A. Zakharov, Gemmy gosudarstvennogo istoricheskogo muzeja (Moscow, 1928), Pl. II: 92; and Legrain, op. cit., Pl. XLVIII:1047; to either side of a ribbon-decorated altar (previously cited in n. 38).

58. Smirnov, op. cit., p. 38; he cites the following seals in Horn and Steindorff, Pl. II:1168 (lion with cross above) and 1153 (lion with Arabic inscription). Cf. Bivar, Pl. 28:

NG 9 (device with cross above crescent). Certainly, the Greek cross with short perpendicular terminations appears conspicuously on early Byzantine seals with New Testament subjects: rock crystal intaglios of the Adoration of the Magi (DOC I, No. 114) and of the Entry into Jerusalem, with Christ led by an angel in the manner of an imperial adventus (Dalton, BAA, fig. 405 and Engraved Gems, Pl. XVIII:549).

59. Bivar, Pl. 10:DD 1.

60. H.H. Von der Osten, "The Ancient Seals from the Near East in the Metropolitan Museum: Old and Middle Persian", The Art Bulletin, XIII (1931), fig. 133; the two small crosses suggest to him Christian ownership (p. 233).

61. Lukonin, No. 195.

62. Horn and Steindorff, Pl. II: 2168.

63. Also, the seal cited in n. 54 and loc. cit., No. 335.

64. For example, Lukonin, No. 23; Bivar, Pl. 7:CC 1-5 and 12 and supra, n. 62.

65. Smirnov identifies the cross on 24* as that erected on Golgotha and sees the couple as a family in prayer before it (op. cit., p. 37).

66. Bivar, Pl. 4:BB 1 and 4.

67. Ibid., pp. 24-5. He also includes seals with full-length figures, especially a seal which shows a man and a woman seated together on a couch, holding a ribboned wreath or diadem between them (Pl. 8: CF 2).

68. Thus, Ardashīr I and his son Shāpūr I, and Bahrām II and his wife and son. See R. Göbl, "Die Münzprägung des Sāsānidenreiches", Vox Orientis, III (1953), pp. 2-3.

69. E. Kantorowicz, "On the Golden Marriage Belt and the Marriage Rings of the Dumbarton Oaks Collection", Dumbarton Oaks Papers, XIV (1960), pp. 1-16.

70. Profile busts: Dalton, Guide, fig. 31 (No. 207); C. Drury Fortnum, "On Finger-Rings of the Early Christian Period", The Archaeological Journal, XXVIII (1871), No. 33; DOC II, Nos. 50-52. Frontal busts: ibid., Nos. 4, 67 and 68 (Nos. 4 and 67 in Kantorowicz, op. cit., fig. 27 a and b).

71. Chabouillet, op. cit., p. 191, and thus accepted by E. Babelon, Guide illustré au Cabinet de Médailles et antiques de la Bibliothèque Nationale: Les Antiques et les objets d'art (Paris, 1900), p. 38.

72. King, Antique Gems and Rings, II, p. 45 and idem, The Gnostics, p. 237.

73. Two women holding between them what seems to be a parasol appear on at least two seals in the British Museum (Bivar, Pl. 8: CG 5) and in Berlin (Horn and Steindorff, Pl. II: 1111). Their attitude differs from those in 25*-27*, and the appearance of a man and a woman with a parasol between them on a seal in Berlin shows this to be a different iconographic type (ibid., Pl. II:265). Nor do the two women on a seal in the Louvre conform to the motif of our seals; although their heads face, their bodies turn away rather than confront each other (Delaporte, Louvre II, Pl. 111: 19). On a late Sasanian silver bowl, two women meet in order for one to offer the other a ribboned ring; the inclusion of this object, among other factors, gives this scene a purely Sasanian meaning with no Christian connotations (R. Ettinghausen, "A Case of Traditionalism in Iranian Art", Forschungen zur Kunst Asiens: In Memoriam Kurt Erdmann [Istanbul, 1970], p. 97, fig. 11).

74. Grabar, Iconography, p. 131; idem, Martyrium, II, pp. 180, 238-42.

75. DACL XV, col. 3132; Lexikon II, cols. 230-31

76. Grabar, Ampoules, Monza No. 2 (Pl. V) and Bobbio fragments 17 and 18 (Pls. XLVI-XLVIII). Also, the sixth-century gold

amulet from Adana, _infra_, no. 95.

77. Lukonin, No. 180.

78. Bivar, Pl. 8:CD 1.

79. Thus, _Lexikon_ I, cols. 545-56, fig. 1 (fourth-century sar-
    cophagus, Vatican); R. Garrucci, _Storia della arte cristi-
    ana_, VI (Prato, 1881), Pl. 486:5 (bronze medallion found
    near Rome); _Survey_ IV, Pl. 248N (sixth-century enamelled
    cross in the Vatican); _DOC_ II, No. 36 (late sixth-century
    gold encolpium from Constantinople).

80. The isolation of the Virgin and Child - not in our form but
    as the seated _Hodegetria_ - from the context of the
    Adoration of the Magi and its transformation into a separate
    iconic type apparently had occurred by the fifth century in
    Egypt from whence it spread to Syria and then to the Latin
    West (V. Lasareff, "Studies in the Iconography of the
    Virgin", _The Art Bulletin_, II [1938], pp. 49-50; also M.
    Werner, "The 'Madonna and Child' Miniature in the Book of
    Kells, Part I", _The Art Bulletin_, LIV [1972], p. 1, n. 3).
    This use in the Christian East of part of a scene to repre-
    sent the whole is a characteristic phenomenon of ancient
    Near Eastern art.

81. GL 482 and 872; both are circular bezels of carnelian and
    banded agate, respectively, and both are unpublished.

82. E.H. Kantorowicz, "The King's Advent' and the Enigmatic
    Panels in the Doors of Santa Sabina", _The Art Bulletin_,
    XXVI (1944), pp. 215-20; Grabar, _Iconography_, pp. 13 and
    44-5.

83. John XII:12-13.

84. Wessel, _op. cit._, Pl. 96.

85. _DACL_ V, col. 52, fig. 4079; E. Babelon, "Intaille sur cor-
    naline, représentant l'entrée du Christ à Jérusalem",
    Bulletin de la Societé nationale des antiquaires de France,
    LVII (1806), line drawing on p. 194.

86. Dalton, Engraved Gems, Pl. XVIII:56; DACL I, col. 2064, fig. 606.

87. Grabar, Iconography, fig. 204.

88. Bivar, Pl. 7:BL 5 and 6.

89. Lexikon I, col. 596.

90. Bivar, Pl. 7:BL 2.

91. C. Diehl, Ravenna (Paris, 1907), illustration on p. 98. In the adventus-type of Entry on a seal in the British Museum (supra, n. 58) the identical type of cross is prominently displayed in the field before the mounted Christ; but on a sixth-century terra-cotta token, of probably Syrian origin, the mounted Christ, greeted by the angel, appears to hold a staff that ends in a cross (the token, one of a hoard of such disks representing various Christian scenes was recently acquired by the Department of Medieval and Later Antiquities of the British Museum. I wish to thank Mr. Richard Camber of the Department for generously making photographs of the tokens available to me).

92. Matthew XXI:8; Mark XI:8.

93. Bonner, op. cit., pp. 87-90

94. A nimbate rider spearing a hydra-like monster is a motif found on some Sasanian seals (e.g. Bivar, Pl. 7: BL 3 and 4); in a future article, I hope to explore this subject and its relation to the "rider-god" of the West (cf. ibid., p. 27).

95. Grabar, Iconography, p. 98 and fig. 248 (two gold amulets from Adana in eastern Asia Minor, probably of the sixth century; the one showing scenes from the life of Christ depicts the Entry in the center of the middle register).

96. Ibid. pp. 10-11.

97. Loc. cit.; K. Weitzmann, "The Question of the Influence of

Jewish Pictorial Sources on Old Testament Illustration",
Studies in Classical and Byzantine Manuscript Illumination
ed. H.L. Kessler (Chicago and London, 1971), pp. 76ff
(trans. of "Zur Frage des Einflusses jüdischer Bilderquel-
len auf die Illustration des Alten Testamentes", Mullus:
Festschrift Theodor Klausner [Jahrbuch für Antike und
Christentum Erganzungsband, I, Münster, 1964], pp. 401ff);
E. Goodenough, Jewish Symbols in the Greco-Roman Period, I
(New York, 1954), p. 266; Bonner, op. cit., pp. 226-27;
and T. Klauser, "Studien zur Entstehungsgeschichte der
Christlichen Kunst, IV", Jahrbuch für Antike und Christentum, IV (1961), pp. 142-44, for the reliance on Jewish
seal rings for Old Testament representations on Christian
gems.

98. Thus, Horn and Steindorff, p. 5 (Nos. 1078-80); Delaporte,
Louvre II, p. 226 (A.1437 and A.1442); M.I. Makhsimova,
"Gemmy iz nekropolja Mtskhety-Samtavro", Vestnik
Gosudarstvennogo Muzeja Gruzii, XVI-B (1950), p. 271 (No.
65N); Lukonin, pp. 101-2 (Nos. 154-58); Bivar, pp. 57 (BD
5), 58 (BD 16) and 66 (CG 3). In his Siegelkanon, p. 37,
Göbl classifies as "Isaaks Opferung" (type 4d) only 31*
(that identified as Abraham's sacrifice of Isaac by
Chabouillet) and others - our 32*, 42* and 48 - as
"Priester mit Altar und Widder" (type 4c).

99. For example, ibid., type 4b.

100. Chabouillet, op. cit., p. 191, and followed by DACL VIII,
col. 1573 (No. 70), and E. Babelon, Le Cabinet des Médailles et Antiquités de la Bibliothèque Nationale. Notice
historique et guide du visiteur. I: Les Antiques et les
objets d'art (Paris, 1924), p. 57 (No. 1330). Smirnov was
not convinced that the seal depicts Abraham, even though
he recognized the child on the altar (op. cit., p. 37).
Rather, he felt that it was too much like other Sasanian
gems with scenes of sacrifice, citing 41, 47 and 48. Our
argument is that these seals are too much like 31* to dis-

miss the identification. For a discussion of Zoroastrian rites of animal sacrifice, see M. Boyce, "Haoma, Priest of the Sacrifice", W.B. Henning Memorial Volume (London, 1970), pp. 68-69.

101. Also pointed out by Bonner, op. cit., p. 311.

102. For example, Ghirshman, Persian Art, pp. 140-41, 146, 157-58; Göbl, supra, n. 68; idem, "Numismatica Byzantino-Persica", Jahrbuch der Österreichischen Byzantinischen Gesellschaft, XVII (1968), pp. 166-67; H. Luschey, "Iran und der Westen von Kyros bis Khosrow", Archäologische Mitteilungen aus Iran, N.F. I (1968), pp. 32-34.

103. This concept and the importance of the Sacrifice of Isaac in Christian liturgy is discussed by I. Speyart van Woerden, "The Iconography of the Sacrifice of Abraham", Vigiliae Christinae, XV (1961), pp. 215-20.

104. DACL VII, cols. 1555-57 and fig. 5974 for the scene in the left niche of the Capella Greca in the Cemetery of Priscilla. See ibid., cols. 1558-61 for a list of the other catacomb paintings where Mount Moriah is depicted.

105. An apparently complete listing of all monuments, including our 31* but not the other Sasanian seals, is given by Speyart van Woerden, op. cit., pp. 214ff, especially the catalogue on pp. 243-51. An earlier, but not so complete, discussion is that of A.M. Smith, "The Iconography of the Sacrifice of Isaac in Early Christian Art", American Journal of Archaeology, XXVI (1922), pp. 159-73.

106. Ibid., fig. 3; A. Fakhry, The Necropolis of el-Bagawāt in the Kharga Oasis (Cairo, 1951), Pls. XXf. The fresco belongs to the fifth century.

107. The pyxides date to the fifth and sixth centuries: Dalton, BAA, fig. 115; W.F. Volbach, Elfenbeinarbeiten der Spätantike und des frühen Mittelalters (Mainz, 1952), Pl. 53: Nos. 162 (Trier), 163 (Bologna) and 164 (Rome, Terme Museum). A widespread belief in the fifth and sixth centu-

ries held that the sacrifice did not take place on Mount
Moriah but on Golgotha which was ascended by steps. Hence
the altars on these pyxides are placed at the top of a
flight of stairs (Ainalov, op. cit., pp. 97-9).

108. On the coinage from the reign of Shāpūr I (241-272) into
that of Khusrō I (531-579), see Göbl, Sasanian Numismatics
Pls. 2-12. Portions of such altars were found at Takht-i
Suleiman (R. Naumann, "Sasanidische Feueraltare", Iranica
Antiqua, VII [1967], fig. 4 and Pl. X: 1 and 2).

109. Siegelkanon, type 98a ("Altar"); type 4b and 4h
("Priester").

110. K. Weitzmann, "The Survival of Mythological Representa-
tions in Early Christian and Byzantine Art and Their
Impact on Christian Iconography", Dumbarton Oaks Papers,
XIV (1960), p. 58. Also H.-J. Geischer, "Heidenische Pa-
rallelen zum Frühchristlichen Bild des Isaak-Opfers",
Jahrbuch für Antike und Christentum, X (1967), pp. 142-44.

111. Speyart van Woerden, op. cit., pp. 243-51 for a list of
such monuments. However, she states that beginning with
the Theodosian sarcophagi of the late fourth century,
Isaac lies upon the altar; in actuality, he only kneels.
See also H.-G. Severin, "Oströmische Reliefs mit Darstel-
lungen des Abrahamsopfers", Bulletin du Musée Hongrois des
Beaux-Arts, XXXVI (1971), pp. 29-46.

112. C.H. Kraeling, The Excavations at Dura-Europos...Final
Report, VIII:1: The Synagogue (New Haven, 1956), Pl. XVI.

113. Makhsimova, op. cit., p. 271; see No. 62 for the Byzantine
ring.

114. The identification as Daniel for these Sasanian seals was
suggested by Smirnov only for certain occurrences of the
figure between lions (op. cit., p. 44), but was made for
the seals in their respective collections by Lukonin, p.
107 (56*) and Bivar, p. 67 (58*). Göbl simply places the
subject (illustrated by 58*) in his category of "Sonstige

Gottheit; König; Fürst; Dignitar; Beamter; Adorant mit zu-
geordnetem Tier (oder Tieren)" (Siegelkanon, 2d). J.B.
Segal identifies the figure as Leon-Atargatis-Hera, yet
acknowledges the similarity with Armenian and Coptic representations of Daniel ("A Syrian Seal Inscription",
Iraq, XXVIII [1966], p. 15 and n. 65).

115. Lexikon IX, cols. 469-73; DACL IV, cols. 224-48; Grabar,
Iconography, figs. 1 and 26.

116. Goodenough, op. cit., IX, p. 158, n. 258

117. Grabar, Iconography, fig. 29.

118. DACL, VI, fig. 5068 and Klauser, op. cit., fig. 6e and
p. 140.

119. DACL VI, fig. 5069 and Klauser, op. cit., fig. 6d.

120. On a fragmentary marble relief: R. Stillwell (ed.),
Antioch-on-the-Orontes, III: The Excavations, 1937-1939
(Princeton, 1941), Pl. 17:368.

121. Furtwängler, op. cit., Pl. LXVII:1

122. Dalton, BAA, fig. 72 (sacrophagus panel): F.W. Deichmann,
Frühchristliche Bauten und Mosaiken von Ravenna (Wiesba-
den, 1958), fig. 82 (stucco decoration in the Orthodox
Baptistry).

123. Volbach, op. cit., Pl. 54: Nos. 167 (British Museum) and
168 (Dumbarton Oaks).

124. Bivar, Pl. 5:BE 1; Segal, op. cit., Pl. IV:a.

125. Ibid., pp. 14-5.

126. The plate was found in the Perm region (Ainalov, op. cit.,
fig. 117); the relief is carved on a chancel from a church
near Salamieh (J. Nasrallah, "Bas-reliefs chrétiens in-
connus de Syrie", Syria, XXXVIII [1961], Pl. III:3).

127. G. Schlumberger, Sigillographie de l'Empire byzantine
(Paris, 1884), p. 26:1; G. Zacos and A. Veglery, Byzantine

Lead Seals (Basel, 1972), Pl. 201: 2960 and 2961.

128. H. Frankfort, Cylinder Seals (London, 1939), Pl. XXXVI, g
     and l (the combatant on the latter is a four-winged ge-
     nius); E. Porada, Corpus of Ancient Near Eastern Seals in
     North American Collections, I. The Collection of the
     Pierpont Morgan Library (New York, 1948), Pl. CXVI:768-69.

129. H.H. Von der Osten, Ancient Oriental Seals in the Collect-
     ion of Mrs. Agnes Baldwin Brett ("Oriental Institute Pub-
     lications", XXXVII, Chicago, 1936), Pl. XII: 138; D.J.
     Wiseman, Cylinder Seals of Western Asia (London, n.d.),
     No. 105 (London WA 89337). This second seals shows both
     the Achaemenid king fighting a lion and an uncrowned man
     fighting a bull. It is interesting to note that for free-
     dom of movement, the king has rolled the wide sleeves of
     his candys to his shoulders in the manner of Daniel on 57*.

130. Bivar, Pl. 8:CG 1 and 2; Legrain, op. cit., Pl. XXXV:737.

131. Daniel VI:22. Smirnov interpreted Daniel's orant posture
     as his strangling the lions of lifting them up to God so
     that his angel would close their mouths.

132. It is possible that the motif of the lion-tamer went out
     of fashion after the Achaemenid period. Von der Osten
     suggests that the subjects of the Assyrian seals may still
     have been in use in Mesopotamia during Parthian times("The
     Ancient Seals from the Near East", p. 231), and among the
     sparse evidence for Parthian glyptic art, certain ancient
     themes do continue. However, much of this carry-over is
     through Achaemenid art; unfortunately, too little is known
     about Parthian seal designs to distinguish survivals in
     Parthian Mesopotamia of traditional indigenous motifs from
     more Persian (i.e. Achaemenid) motifs in Parthian Iran; in
     fact, we cannot be certain that such distinctions even ob-
     tain. An Iranian hero fighting a winged lion occurs on a
     seal impression from Parthian Nisa in Turkmenistan (M.E.
     Masson and G.A. Pugachenkova, "Ottiski parfjanskikh

pechatej iz Nisy", <u>Vestnik drevnej istorii</u>, IV [1954],
fig. 1), but the theme was no longer popular by Sasanian
times. It may indeed have been eclipsed during the Parthian period by images of the lion-taming Herakles, whose
cult was popular in Iran, and of whom a seal impression
from Seleucid - though perhaps Parthian - Babylon is known
(F. Wetzel, <u>et al</u>., <u>Das Babylon der Spätzeit</u> ["Wissen-
schaftliche Veröffentlichungen der Deutschen Orient-
Gesellschaft", 62, Berlin, 1957], Pl. 40, h; the Parthian
attribution of the bulla, though not necessarily of the
seal itself, was offered by A.D.H. Bivar, "A Parthian
Amulet", <u>Bulletin of the Schools of Oriental and African
Studies</u>, XXX [1967], p. 517)

133. Lukonin, p. 107.

134. Thus, the examples cited in notes 119 and 121. W. Deonna
lists eighteen different positions for the lions and
Daniel and cites objects on which the lions' heads are to
the ground ("Daniel, le 'maître des fauves' à propos d'une
lampe chrétienne du Musée de Genève", <u>Artibus Asiae</u>, XII
[1949], pp. 125-30).

135. <u>Ibid</u>., pp. 366-68.

136. <u>DACL</u> I, fig. 269 and XI, figs. 2780 and 2781; also H.
Kühn, "Die Danielschnallen der Völkerwanderungszeit",
<u>IPEK; Jahrbuch für prähistorische und ethnographische
Kunst</u>, XV-XVI (1941), Pl. 76:52. On the ivory pyxis in the
British Museum, St. Menas, clothed in tight trousers,
tunic and chlamys, is flanked by <u>recumbant</u> camels (Dalton,
<u>Catalogue</u>, Pl. IX,c).

137. Deonna, <u>op</u>. <u>cit</u>., figs. 1-3.

138. Kühn, <u>op</u>. <u>cit</u>., especially Pls. 59-65. Cf. R. Bernheimer,
"A Sasanian Monument in Merovingian France", <u>Ars Islamica</u>,
V (1938), especially pp. 229 and 231-32.

139. E.L. Sukenik, <u>The Ancient Synagogue at Beth-Alpha</u> (Jerusa-

lem, 1932), Pl. XIX. As pointed out by Speyart van Woerden (op. cit., p. 228), the type represented here belongs to no known category; the very primitive excution of the pavement marks it as a local phenomenon - an invention of a local artist.

140. Bonner, op. cit., Pl. XVIII:343. The amulet (or seal), formerly in the collection of C.C. Torrey, has engraved on its reverse four lines of indistinct Hebrew or Aramaic letters. Its Jewish affiliations have been accepted by Kraeling, op. cit., p. 58, no. 130, and Klauser, op. cit., p. 144, although the lettering is a later addition.

141. Cf. M. Schapiro, "The Angel with the Ram in Abraham's Sacrifice: A Parallel in Western and Islamic Art", Ars Islamica, X (1943), p. 140.

142. Goodenough, op. cit., II, p. 224; cf. Geischer, op. cit., p. 143, no. 122.

143. Goodenough, op. cit.; E. Namenyi, L'Esprit de l'art juif (Paris, 1957), p. 40; but see Klauser, op. cit., p. 144.

144. L.H. Vincent, "Le Sanctuaire juif d'ʿAïn Douq", Revue biblique, N.S. XVI (1919), figs. 1 (p. 535) and 2 (p. 538).

145. Goodenough, op. cit., II, pp. 223-24 and III, fig. 1036; the Daniel with lions in fig. 1037 is seen as a Christian- ization of the Jewish theme by the simple inclusion within the Greek legend of a cross with arms of equal length. Cf. Klauser, op. cit.

146. Although there seems to be evidence in the fifth to seventh centuries for the same workshops turning out glass vessels for both Jewish and Christian customers, the mo- tifs on the vessels differ according to the religion of the buyers (Barag, "Glass Pilgrim Vessels from Jerusalem, Parts II and III", p. 45-46). Other vessels which bear "neutral" motifs, i.e., those without obvious Jewish or Christian symbols, nevertheless probably were not used by

members of both religious groups (<u>ibid</u>., p. 51). Even if
these neutral designs were shared, it seems unlikely that
two specific Old Testament subjects - and only these two -
were used by both Jews and Christians on objects so personal as seals. Significantly there are no motifs on seals
of the Sasanian period that can be identified as Jewish
(e.g. menorah, incense shovel, shofar and lulav) and would
thus correspond to those seals with crosses and New Testament scenes.

147. C. Roth, "Jewish Antecedents of Christian Art", <u>Journal of
the Warburg and Courtauld Institutes</u>, XVI (1953), pp. 24ff,
esp. pp. 32-33; H. Stern, "Quelques problèmes d'iconogra-
phie paléo-chrétienne et juive", <u>Cahiers archéologiques</u>,
XII (1962), pp. 112-13. Weitzmann has assumed that a pictorial imagery was developed to illustrate Jewish texts as
early as Hellenistic times, although concrete evidence of
Jewish book illustration is still wanting ("The Influence
of Jewish Pictorial Sources", esp. pp. 81-82 and 94-95;
<u>idem</u>, "The Illustration of the Septuagint", Studies in
Classical and Byzantine Manuscript Illumination, pp, 71,
74- [trans. of "Die Illustration der Septuaginta", <u>Münch-
ner Jahrbuch der bildenden Kunst</u>, 3/4 (1952/53), pp. 96-
120]. Certainly, evidence exists that illustrations of Old
Testament scenes were based on Jewish <u>literary</u> descript-
ions (or upon oral traditions), exclusive of corresponding
representational ones. Thus, Schapiro, <u>op</u>. <u>cit</u>., and <u>idem</u>,
"An Irish-Latin Text on the Angel with the Ram in Abra-
ham's Sacrifice", <u>Essays in the History of Art Presented
to Rudolf Wittkower</u>, ed. D. Fraser, (New York, 1967), pp.
17ff. Cf. J. Gutmann, "The Illustrated Jewish Manuscript
in Antiquity: the Present State of the Question", <u>Gesta</u>, V
(1966), pp. 39-44.

148. For a discussion of the hybrid nature of Durene art and
its relationship to that of Mesopotamia, see A. Perkins,
<u>The Art of Dura-Europos</u> (Oxford, 1973), pp. 117-18.

149. Nasrallah has suggested that the Christian sculptor of the Syrian chancel relief had wanted to create a Daniel to resemble the legendary Babylonian hero, Gilgamesh (op. cit., p. 49).

150. Waves of persecution plagued Christian communities under Sasanian control throughout the reign of the dynasty. Yet the last century of Sasanian rule saw the expansion of Christianity in Iran (Frye, Heritage of Persia, pp. 214-15 and 228; also P. Devos, "Les Martyrs persans à travers leurs actes syriaques", La Persia e il mondo greco-romano ['Accademia nazionale dei Lincei", 76, Rome, 1966], pp. 213-25, and the sources cited in n. 1, as well as Ericsson, op. cit.).

151. Cf. J. Beckwith, "Early Christian Art, The Eastern Provinces of the Empire and Byzantium", Tardo antico e alto medioevo, La Forma artistica nel passaggio dell'antichità al medioevo ("Accademia nazionale dei Lincei", 365, Rome, 1968), pp. 223ff.

152. Particularly for the jewelled cross, Syria offers numerous examples. See J. Leroy, Les Manuscrits syriaques à peintures conservés dans les bibliothèques d'Europe et d'Orient, I (Paris, 1964), p. 116.

153. The use of the cross without the crucifixion as an apotropaion is discussed by Grabar, Martyrium, II. pp. 277-90. Its use in Syria and Egypt is noted by Leroy (op. cit., p. 113 and n. 1) and P. Nautin ("La Conversion du Temple de Philae en eglise chrétienne", Cahiers archéologiques, XVII [1967], pp. 15-16 and 35-38), respectively.

154. This increase in the use of seals surely begins by the late fifth century, for it is probably associated with the administrative and fiscal reforms of Kavād I (484; 488-497; 499-531). The proliferation of seals from the time of his son, Khusrō I (531-579) continues this response to the

new laws and requirements (cf. Christensen, op. cit., pp.
366ff).

155. For example, the provincial Roman character of the stucco
saint from Ctesiphon which differs greatly in style from
our seals with their Syrian and Sasanian characteristics
(Meyer, op. cit., fig. 13).

LIST OF ILLUSTRATIONS

Collection).
Photo: author's impression.

Seal 19*. Figure holding a cross (?).
Photo: Trustees of the British Museum.

Seal 20*. Male figure in prayer (M. Foroughi Collection).
Photo: author's impression.

Seal 22*. Male figure in orant posture (Museum für Islamische Kunst).
Photo: author's impression.

Seal 23*. Male orant (S.Y. Nayeri Collection).
Photo: Frye, "Inscribed Seals from the Nayeri Collection", Fig. 7.

Seal 24*. Confronted busts of a couple adoring the cross (Bibliothèque Nationale).
Photo: author's impression.

Seal 25*. The Visitation (Bibliothèque Nationale).
Photo: author's impression.

Seal 26* The Visitation.
Photo: Metropolitan Museum of Art.

Seal 27*. The Visitation (M. Foroughi Collection).
Photo: R.N. Frye.

Seal 28*. Virgin and Child: the Adoration (Bibliothèque Nationale).
Photo: author's impression.

Seal 29*. The Entry into Jerusalem (M. Foroughi Collection).
Photo: author's impression.

Seal 30*. The Entry into Jerusalem (Harvard Semitic Museum).
Photo: author's impression.

Seal 31*. The Sacrifice of Isaac (Bibliothèque Nationale).
Photo: author's impression.

Seal 32*. The Sacrifice of Isaac (Bibliothèque Nationale).
Photo: author's impression.

Seal 33*. The Sacrifice of Isaac (Hermitage Museum).
Photo: author's impression.

Seal 36*. The Sacrifice of Isaac (Ashmolean Museum).
Photo: author's impression.

Seal 37*. The Sacrifice of Isaac (Kunsthistorisches Museum).
Photo: author's impression.

Seal 38*. The Sacrifice of Isaac (Hermitage Museum).
Photo: author's impression.

Seal 42*. The Sacrifice of Isaac.
Photo: Trustees of the British Museum.

Seal 44*. The Sacrifice of Isaac.
Photo: Trustees of the British Museum.

Seal 45*. The Sacrifice of Isaac.
Photo: Royal Ontario Museum.

Seal 49*. The Sacrifice of Isaac (Hermitage Museum).
Photo: author's impression.

Seal 50*. The Sacrifice of Isaac (Kunsthistorisches Museum).
Photo: author's impression.

Seal 55*. The Sacrifice of Isaac (Museum of Fine Arts).
Photo: author's impression.

Seal 56*. Daniel in the Lions' Den (Hermitage Museum).
Photo: author's impression.

Seal 57*. Daniel in the Lions' Den (Hermitage Museum).
Photo: author's impression.

Seal 58*. Daniel in the Lions' Den.
Photo: Trustees of the British Museum.

Seal 65*. Daniel in the Lions' Den (Hermitage Museum).
Photo: author's impression.

Figure A. Byzantine Ring (British Museum, Department of
Medieval and Later Antiquities, 67, 7-19, 3).
Photo: Trustees of the British Museum.

Figure B. Coptic painting from Saqqara: orant saint.
Photo: K. Wessel, Koptische Kunst, fig. X.

Figure C. Christian intaglio: the Entry into Jerusalem
(British Museum, Department of Medieval and Later
Antiquities, unregistered). Drawing after photo,
courtesy of the Trustees of the British Museum.

Figure D. Painting from the Torah Shrine of the Synagogue,
Dura-Europos.
Photo: C.H. Kraeling, The Excavations at Dura-
Europos... Final Report, VIII/1: The Synagogue,
Pl. XVI.

Figure E. Seal impression, British Museum, Department of
Western Asiatic Antiquities, 119393.
Photo: Trustees of the British Museum.

PLATES

1

2

3

4

5

6

7

8

9

11

10

12

13

14

15

PLATE III

16

17

18

19

20

21

22

23

24

25

26

27

28

29

30

31

32

33

34

35

36

37

38

39

A

C

B

D

E